STRONG AND COURAGEOUS

TIMELESS TRUTHS TO CONQUER FEAR,
CRUSH ANXIETY, AND DEFEAT DESPAIR
IN AN UNCERTAIN WORLD

A 52-WEEK DEVOTIONAL THROUGH THE BOOK OF JOSHUA

STRONG AND COURAGEOUS

TIMELESS TRUTHS TO CONQUER FEAR, CRUSH ANXIETY, AND DEFEAT DESPAIR IN AN UNCERTAIN WORLD

A 52-WEEK DEVOTIONAL THROUGH THE BOOK OF JOSHUA

DR. THOMAS WHITE

STRONG AND COURAGEOUS © 2025 by Dr. Thomas White.
All rights reserved.

Printed in the United States of America

Published by Igniting Souls
PO Box 43, Powell, OH 43065
IgnitingSouls.com

This book contains material protected under international and federal copyright laws and treaties. Any unauthorized reprint or use of this material is prohibited. No part of this book may be reproduced or transmitted in any form or by any means, electronic or mechanical, including photocopying, recording, or by any information storage and retrieval system, without express written permission from the author.

LCCN: 2025912951
Paperback ISBN: 978-1-63680-540-5
Hardback ISBN: 978-1-63680-541-2
eBook ISBN: 978-1-63680-542-9

Available in paperback, hardcover, e-book, and audiobook.

Scripture quotations from The ESV® Bible (The Holy Bible, English Standard Version®) are notated with ESV. © 2001 by Crossway, a publishing ministry of Good News Publishers. Used by permission. All rights reserved.

Any Internet addresses (websites, blogs, etc.) and telephone numbers printed in this book are offered as a resource. They are not intended in any way to be or imply an endorsement by Igniting Souls, nor does Igniting Souls vouch for the content of these sites and numbers for the life of this book.

Some names and identifying details may have been changed to protect the privacy of individuals.

Dedication

This book is dedicated to my students, past, present, and future. I am unworthy of the honor to serve you and point you toward King Jesus. Thank you for allowing me the privilege. Never forget that God is faithful.
We can trust Him.

Scan the QR code or visit cedarville.edu/Joshua-Devotional to access additional study resources including Thomas White's chapel messages from the book of Joshua, free Bible courses from Cedarville's world-class faculty, and more.

Table of Contents

11	A Note to You—The Reader	
13	Introduction	
15	Every Single Word	(Josh 21:45; 23:14)
19	Moses, My Servant	(Josh 1:1, 2, 7, 13, 15)
23	Just as He Promised	(Josh 1:3, 6; 6:5, 20)
27	Be Strong and Courageous	(Josh 1:6, 7, 9, 18)
31	Meditate on It Day and Night	(Josh 1:7-8)
35	The Lord Will Be with You	(Josh 1:5, 9, 17; 6:27)
39	Do Not Be Frightened or Dismayed	(Josh 1:9; 8:1; 10:8; 11:6)
43	The Faith of Rahab	(Josh 2:9-11; 6:23-25)
47	The Scarlet Thread of Redemption	(Josh 2:18, 21)

51	No Water Too Deep or Too Wide	(Josh 3:13, 15-17; 4:18)
55	On Dry Ground	(Josh 3:17; 4:18, 22)
59	Twelve Stones	(Josh 4:3, 6-7, 9, 20-24)
63	The Lord Exalts	(Josh 3:7; 4:14)
67	Fear of the Lord	(Josh 4:24; 5:1)
71	Time to Obey	(Josh 5:5-7, 9; 6:14)
75	No More Manna	(Josh 5:10-12)
79	Sword Drawn: Are You on God's Side?	(Josh 5:13-15)
83	The Best-Laid Plans	(Josh 6:3-5)
87	Devoted Things	(Josh 6:18; 7:1, 11, 13; 10:28)
91	A Curse Fulfilled	(Josh 6:26)
95	Get UP!	(Josh 7:10, 8:1)
99	Trouble in the Valley	(Josh 7:24, 26)
103	Contrasting Faith: Achan vs. Rahab	(Josh 2-7)
107	Victory After Defeat	(Josh 8:8, 18, 34-35)
111	Uncut Stones	(Josh 8:30-31)

115	Self-Sufficiency, Deception, and Prayerless Decisions	(Josh 9:14)
119	Keeping Your Word	(Josh 9:18)
123	Tragedy Into Triumph	(Josh 10:6-9, 42)
127	When God Acts	(Josh 10:11-14; 19, 39)
131	Joshua Obeyed	(Josh 11:9, 12, 15, 23)
135	The Lord Controls All	(Josh 11:20)
139	Failure to Conquer	(Josh 13:1, 13)
143	Balaam Dies	(Josh 13:22)
147	Wholly Followed God	(Josh 14:8-9, 14)
151	Unfinished Task	(Josh 15:63; 16:10; 17:12; 17:16, 18)
155	Daughters	(Josh 17:3-4)
159	Ungrateful & Entitled	(Josh 18:3)
163	Justice and Mercy	(Josh 20:3-4, 9)
167	Living Among the People	(Josh 21:3, 41-42)
171	God Keeps His Promises	(Josh 21:43-45)
175	Turn and Go: Wisdom for Living	(Josh 22:4-6)

179	Misunderstandings	(Josh 22:12, 16, 22-28, 30-31)
183	What About Our Children?	(Josh 22:24)
187	A Legacy of Faithful Witness	(Josh 22:26-27, 28, 34)
191	Be Strong and Careful	(Josh 23:6-13)
195	The Way of All the Earth	(Josh 23:14; 24:29-32)
199	Shechem—A Memorable Place	(Josh 24:1; Gen 12:6-7)
203	Put Away Other Gods	(Josh 24:14b)
207	You Are Not Able!	(Josh 24:19, 22, 27)
211	Choose Whom You Will Serve	(Josh 24:14-15)
215	The Bones of Joseph	(Josh 24:32; Ex 13:19; Gen 50:22-26)
219	Three Funerals and One Great Hope	(Josh 24:29-30)
223	Endnotes	
225	About the Author	

A Note to You—The Reader

Fear. Anxiety. Despair.

We've all felt them. We've all let them keep us from speaking up when we should have. We've all let those emotions keep us on the sidelines when we need to get into the game.

So, how do we conquer our emotions and respond with strong and courageous faith?

Joshua.

I wish I had studied this book earlier. I'm more confident than ever that Joshua knew these emotions. He felt them. He followed Moses, whom the Bible called one of the greatest leaders of all time. Joshua had to lead millions of people across a flooded Jordan River, take a nomadic people to war against established cities, and defeat trained warriors with chariots. Humanly speaking, he had no chance. At one moment in this book, he is face down on the ground.

Fear. Anxiety. Despair.

How do we overcome them?

I hope you will join me on a little journey. We aren't going to cross the Jordan or go to war against human armies. But we will learn the secret to strong and courageous faith. Like any muscle, faith must be challenged and exercised to grow stronger. This journey has fifty-two devotions. You can do one a day or one a week. It will take time, but if you dedicate yourself to the journey, your faith will grow stronger.

At the end of each devotion, we will have an assignment. We call these courageous steps. With each step, my prayer is that your faith grows stronger and more courageous. Read through each devotion at your own pace, and then take the recommended step to grow your faith.

Lord willing, after this journey, you will see how Joshua conquered his fear, anxiety, and despair. Lord willing, after this journey, you will conquer your own fear, anxiety, and despair through strong and courageous faith.

Are you ready? Okay, let's go.

Introduction

I long to see a generation respond to God's promises and presence with strong and courageous faith. I pray that these devotions help accomplish this goal, but I wanted to tell you a little about how this project developed. If you aren't interested in that, then feel free to skip to the first devotion.

These devotions flow from a sermon series preached on the campus of Cedarville University during the 2024-25 school year. You can find them online. The title of that series was "Every Single Word." You'll find that title for one of the devotions. It highlights that the book emphasizes how God kept every single promise, but because that title has to be explained, we went with *Strong and Courageous* for this project.

In the course of study and preparation, I consulted many commentaries and other preachers. I am indebted to a new commentary from Jason Lee and Randy McKinion, who teach at Cedarville. I also found the works of Dale Ralph Davis, Warren Wiersbe, and James Montgomery Boice particularly helpful. You will see their influences through various thoughts and words throughout.

Having read through ten commentaries for each sermon, internalizing their thoughts and preaching through each verse in Joshua, I am no longer sure which thoughts are mine or others. Solomon told us long ago that there is nothing new under the sun.

After writing and developing these devotions, I did something new for me. I used Artificial Intelligence as my first editor. I needed to learn more about AI since many of my students use it on a regular basis. I accepted some suggestions and rejected others, learning a lot in the process. Kary Oberbrunner and his team at Igniting Souls, Rachel Benefiel, and the Cedarville Marketing and Communications team all made this project better. Any faults that remain are mine alone.

The purpose of these devotions is to lead the reader closer to Christ. This is not an academic exercise or intended to impress anyone with prosaic excellence or formal style. The purpose is real spiritual growth. I pray that if I have written anything unhelpful, it will be quickly forgotten, but if anything in these pages is consistent with scripture and glorifies God, the Spirit will imprint it on our minds and hearts.

At Cedarville, it is our desire to stand for the Word of God and the Testimony of Jesus Christ. I welcome you to come visit us. Check out our chapel sermons or Bible Minor (for free) online, and send any college-age students our way as we seek to transform lives through excellent education and intentional discipleship in submission to biblical authority.

Every Single Word

Joshua 21:45: "Not one word of all the good promises that the Lord had made to the house of Israel had failed; all came to pass."

Joshua 23:14: "And now I am about to go the way of all the earth, and you know in your hearts and souls, all of you, that not one word has failed of all the good things that the Lord your God promised concerning you. All have come to pass for you; not one of them has failed."

Final words are important.

When Joshua gave his final words, he reflected on a lifetime of witnessing God's faithfulness. From the Exodus to the Promised Land, not one single promise God made fell short. Think about that—every single word came to pass.

Consider your own life. How often do doubts creep in and stir anxiety? Much of our worry stems from a lack of trust in God's promises. Yet scripture reminds us time and again of His unwavering faithfulness. Trust the testimony of Joshua.

Trust God's Word. God has proven that He is faithful, and we can trust Him.

What promises resonate with you today? Here are a few to hold on to:

- **Psalm 34:18**: "The Lord is near to the brokenhearted and saves the crushed in spirit."
- **Matt. 28:20b**: "And behold, I am with you always, to the end of the age."
- **John 3:16**: "For God so loved the world, that he gave his only Son, that whoever believes in him should not perish but have eternal life."
- **John 16:33**: "I have said these things to you, that in me you may have peace. In the world you will have tribulation. But take heart; I have overcome the world."
- **Romans 8:30-31**: "And those whom he predestined he also called, and those whom he called he also justified, and those whom he justified he also glorified. What then shall we say to these things? If God is for us, who can be against us?"
- **Romans 8:37-39**: "No, in all these things we are more than conquerors through him who loved us. For I am sure that neither death nor life, nor angels nor rulers, nor things present nor things to come, nor powers, nor height nor depth, nor anything else in all creation, will be able to separate us from the love of God in Christ Jesus our Lord."

If God is with us and for us, who can stand against us? Nothing will ever separate us from His love. Nothing!

Remember, God called you, God justified you, and God has glorified you. Even though glorification is a future promise, it's so certain that Paul describes it as if it's already happened. We must trust that one day, God will glorify us and make all things new. We will live with Him forever.

With these truths in mind, let's live with the same strong and courageous faith as Joshua, knowing that "every single word" of God's promises will come to pass.

> **COURAGEOUS STEP:**
>
> God keeps every single promise. Write down one promise of God that you need to remember during your current season. Keep it where you'll see it daily, and choose to trust that not one word of God's promises will fail.

Moses, My Servant

Joshua 1:2a: "Moses my servant is dead."

Have you ever pondered what people might say about you after you're gone? While this thought can be somber, it's important to recognize that the person we will become tomorrow is shaped by who we are today. In other words, the way we live now will determine the legacy we leave behind.

Consider the significance of this in the book of Joshua.

The opening words God speaks to Joshua are profound: "Moses my servant is dead."

Throughout the book, Moses is repeatedly referred to as "the servant of the Lord." This title is emphasized over ten times, a clear reflection of its importance. Joshua does not receive this title until after his death. In both Joshua 24:29 and Judges 2:8, he is then called, "Joshua . . . the servant of the Lord."

What about you? What titles are you striving for in your life? Perhaps you desire a college degree, a certain job title, or roles like "husband," "wife," "mom," "dad," "grandpa," "grandma," or "retired." These aspirations are valid, but they often come with patience and waiting. Yet there is one title that anyone can embrace right now: "servant of the Lord."

At first glance, the title "servant" might seem less glamorous. But Jesus redefined greatness in Matthew 20:25–28: "But Jesus called them to him and said, 'You know that the rulers of the Gentiles lord it over them, and their great ones exercise authority over them. It shall not be so among you. But whoever would be great among you must be your servant, and whoever would be first among you must be your slave, even as the Son of Man came not to be served but to serve, and to give his life as a ransom for many.'"

Reflect also on Philippians 2:3–5: "Do nothing from selfish ambition or conceit, but in humility count others more significant than yourselves. Let each of you look not only to his own interests, but also to the interests of others. Have this mind among yourselves, which is yours in Christ Jesus."

Jesus exemplified perfect servanthood, humbling Himself even to the point of death on a cross. He came to serve, not to be served. If we seek to follow Christ, then "servant of the Lord" should be the title we most desire.

Today, how can you embody this spirit of service? Can you choose words that uplift rather than criticize? Can you presume the best in others instead of the worst? Can you extend grace to those who offend you rather than seeking retribution? Can you welcome those on the fringes or offer friendship to the lonely? Can you stay humble and direct glory to God rather than seeking it for yourself? Can you be the hands and feet of Jesus in your community?

Every day, strive to be a faithful steward of what God has entrusted to you. In doing so, you too can earn the cherished title of "servant of the Lord."

COURAGEOUS STEP:

The greatest title you can aspire to is "servant of the Lord." So today, seek to serve God and others. Write down or, better yet, find a way that you can serve someone humbly in Jesus's name and note how fulfilling serving others can be.

Just as He Promised

Joshua 1:6: "Be strong and courageous, for you shall cause this people to inherit the land that I swore to their fathers to give them."

God made a promise. He swore to give the land to Abraham and his offspring. Think about this promise. Abraham and Sarah were too old to bear children. They had no son. They had no land. Yet God promised to make their descendants as vast as the stars in the sky and to give them a land occupied by mighty cities, warriors, and giant men. What would your reaction be if God promised this to you? "Yeah, right?" "No way?" Or perhaps, "What have you been smoking?"

The book of Joshua starts off by reminding us of these promises. Verse 3 states, "just as I promised to Moses," and verse 6 continues, "the land that I swore to their fathers to give them." Romans 15:4a states, "whatever was written in former days was written for our instruction." The book of Joshua teaches us that God keeps His promises. I remind myself and others frequently that God is faithful, and we can trust Him.

God keeping His promises relies on two variables: Is His character such that He will keep His word? Is His power such that He can?

The Bible teaches us about God's character. It tells us that God "is the same yesterday and today and forever" (Hebrews 13:8). "God is light, and in Him is no darkness at all" (1 John 1:5). Scripture shows us that God displays consistent characteristics, such as grace, mercy, holiness, and judgment. So God's character demonstrates that He will keep His promises.

But is God able? Let's reflect just on Joshua. The rivers of the Jordan stand up so the Israelites can walk across on dry ground (Joshua 3). The walls of Jericho fall flat (Joshua 6). The day lengthens, making the sun appear to stand still at Joshua's prayer (Joshua 10). Hailstones destroy more enemy soldiers than the sword does (Joshua 10). God sends hornets to drive out the enemy rather than the sword or the bow (Joshua 24). The God who created the world and all that is in it through the power of His Word is able.

So what does this mean for us today? Let's remember a few of the promises of God. Some of these we mentioned previously.

- Nothing can separate us from the love of God in Christ Jesus (Romans 8:37–39).
- God will never leave you nor forsake you (Hebrews 13:5).
- The Lord is near to the brokenhearted (Psalm 34:18).
- God will supply our needs (Philippians 4:19).

- God provides rest for the weary (Matthew 11:28–29).
- God will forgive those who repent (1 John 1:9).
- God provides eternal life for those who believe (John 3:16).

The resurrection and restoration of God's creation will solve every problem. As D. A. Carlson said, "I'm not suffering from anything a good resurrection can't fix."

Do you see why God keeping His promises is important? This provides us with genuine hope. We can persevere. We can have genuine joy. Our future is secure. No matter what struggles or problems we face today, we will overcome.

Perhaps you're wondering who to trust. Do you build your life and future on the promises of the world or the promises of God? Will you regret your decision twenty years from now? Will you build the house of your life on the shifting sands this world offers, or will you build the house of your life on the rock, Jesus Christ?

As someone who has traveled around the sun more than fifty times, I plead with you to build your life on the truths of scripture. God has never failed me. Trust in God. Everything in scripture will happen just as He promised.

COURAGEOUS STEP:

You should have already written down a promise that you need. Now memorize the verse associated with that promise. You can write it on a notecard, sticky note, or just write it down repeatedly until you own the promise. Then, claim this promise when doubt and anxiety creep into your life. The Spirit will bring to mind this verse when you struggle with a lack of faith.

Be Strong and Courageous

Joshua 1:9: "Have I not commanded you? Be strong and courageous. Do not be frightened, and do not be dismayed, for the Lord your God is with you wherever you go."

Authors use repetition—let me repeat that—**repetition**—to emphasize a major point. In Joshua 1:6, the author says, *"Be strong and courageous."* He repeats in the next verse, *"Only be strong and very courageous."* Then again, in verse 9, he underscores it. And if three commands in four verses weren't enough, the chapter ends with the people responding to Joshua: *"Only be strong and courageous"* (Joshua 1:18).

But there's more.

In Deuteronomy 31:6, Moses commands the people: *"Be strong and courageous. Do not fear or be in dread of them, for it is the Lord your God who goes with you. He will not leave you or forsake you."* In the next verse, Moses addresses Joshua in the presence of all Israel: *"Be strong and courageous"* and *"Do not fear or be dismayed"* (Deuteronomy 31:8). Later, in Deuteronomy 31:23, the Lord Himself commissioned Joshua: *"Be strong and courageous . . . I will be with you."*

A preacher once said the Bible states "do not fear" 365 times, one for each day of the year. The repeated commands throughout scripture suggest we all wrestle with fear. To be strong and courageous means we choose not to fear.

If you're afraid, you're not alone. We all have fears, some rational, others not. We fear sharing the Gospel. We fear rejection. We fear we won't say the right thing. We fear letting people truly know us. We fear trying something new. We fear failure. We fear what others might think. We fear persecution. It's in our nature to let fear hold us back. But scripture calls us to rise above our fears and step out in bold faith for Jesus.

When fear grips you, remember that you are not alone. Not just because others feel it too, but because **the Lord is with you.** If you've prayed, sought God's will, and believe He's calling you to take the next step—if your actions align with scripture—then God is with you. The outcome doesn't depend on your strength but on His. He is able.

When we humbly obey His call, we can trust Him to carry us through. Our only reasonable response is strong and courageous faith. This is our spiritual act of worship (Romans 12:1–2).

I enjoy country music, especially Garth Brooks. Several of his songs echo the theme of taking a leap of faith. In "The Dance," he sings, "Our lives are better left to chance. I could have missed the pain, but I'd have had to miss the dance." Swap "chance" with God's sovereign will, and you get my point. Following God may not be easy, but it's always worth it.

In "The River," he sings, "Too many times we stand aside and let the waters slip away . . . choose to chance the rapids and dare to dance the tide." Later: "There's bound to be rough waters, and I know I'll take some falls. But with the good Lord as my captain, I can make it through them all." The takeaway? Sail your vessel until the river runs dry.

So, let's choose to live boldly. Let's be strong and courageous. If God is for us, who can be against us? And if we encounter hardship, struggle, or even failure, we are still successful because the ultimate goal of life is to trust and obey God with strong and courageous faith.

That is our calling.

COURAGEOUS STEP:

Fear is common to all humanity, or this command would not be repeated so frequently. Recognize and admit your fear. Write it down. Take one bold action this week that moves forward in faith despite that fear, trusting that God will be with you.

Meditate on It Day and Night

Joshua 1:8: "This Book of the Law shall not depart from your mouth, but you shall meditate on it day and night, so that you may be careful to do according to all that is written in it. For then you will make your way prosperous, and then you will have good success."

No Bible, no breakfast.

That's a phrase I often share with my students. Every morning, I open my Bible program and read from the Old Testament, New Testament, Psalms, and Proverbs. I follow a plan that takes me through the entire Bible in one year. On top of that, I'm usually studying a particular book more deeply—reading it multiple times, consulting commentaries, and memorizing key passages.

Why? Because I want to be prosperous and have good success. But it goes deeper than that. I know how sinful I am. I know that, left unchecked, my heart naturally drifts away from God. If I'm not grounded daily, habitually, in God's Word, I'll lose my way. I've also learned that the more I understand God and myself, the more I grow in love and gratitude for Him. That's why I know I still need to grow, especially in meditating on scripture at night before bed.

In Joshua 1:8, the Lord commands Joshua to keep the Word close—speaking it, discussing it, and meditating on it continually. This "Book of the Law" refers to the first five books of the Old Testament, written by Moses. The call to meditate means more than simply reading a verse or checking off a devotional box. It means thinking deeply, prayerfully considering what God has said and how it applies to our lives.

We're called not only to internalize God's Word but also to **obey it**. Meditation should lead to transformation. We are to be careful in following God's commands. We must live them out in real time, not just admire them in theory.

Is this command only for Joshua? Absolutely not.

- **Psalm 1:2** describes the blessed person as one whose "delight is in the law of the Lord," and who "on his law he meditates day and night."
- **Psalm 119:15** says, "I will meditate on your precepts and fix my eyes on your ways."
- And in **Philippians 4:8**, Paul urges us to think on whatever is true, noble, right, pure, lovely, admirable, excellent, and praiseworthy—in other words, godly principles found in scripture.

If you want to live a strong Christian life, you must meditate on God's Word. If you don't have a reading plan, it's time to get one. If you're not in the Word daily, it's time to develop the habit. Start small, but stay intentional.

Think of it like the activity rings on an Apple Watch.

- **The stand goal** is simply opening your Bible and reading a verse or two. Spiritually speaking, that means you're showing up. You've cracked open your Bible—good! You're alive and breathing.
- **The exercise goal** requires more effort. This might involve deeper study, reflective thinking, or scripture journaling. Your spiritual heart rate goes up.
- **The move goal** takes real engagement. It's when you've not only read and studied but also prayed, applied what you've read, sought God's guidance, and actively served others. Now, we're talking!

When all three "rings" are completed, you've had a spiritually healthy day. But the goal isn't just one good day; it's a **streak**.

One day becomes ten. Ten becomes a month. And over time, you begin to see change. You're more joyful. You're less focused on yourself and more on serving God and others. You find lasting satisfaction from communion with God and not from circumstances.

That's real prosperity. That's true success.

How do we get there? Not through quick fixes or emotional highs, but through **a long, steady walk in the same direction**. We stay the course. We follow Joshua 1:8. We meditate on God's Word day and night. We obey what it says and live it out.

Then, when the final day comes, Resurrection Day, you'll look back with no regrets, knowing yours was a life well-lived in God's strength and truth.

> **COURAGEOUS STEP:**
>
> Commit to a Bible reading plan this month. Start small if needed, but stay consistent. Begin your streak of reading scripture and see how long you can keep it going. No Bible, no breakfast. Let God's Word saturate your heart and guide your steps.

The Lord Will Be with You

Joshua 1:5: "No man shall be able to stand before you all the days of your life. Just as I was with Moses, so I will be with you. I will not leave you or forsake you."

Joshua 1:9: "Have I not commanded you? Be strong and courageous. Do not be frightened, and do not be dismayed, for the Lord your God is with you wherever you go."

We all go through seasons of fear, anxiety, and uncertainty. Maybe you're heading off to college, starting a new job, or navigating the complexities of caring for aging parents. You're not alone in how you feel.

Statistics show that over **1 in 4 members of Generation Z** struggles with anxiety. Among them:

- **51%** feel anxious about making important decisions
- **47%** are afraid of failing
- **45%** feel uncertain about the future[1]

For college students, the numbers are even more sobering:

- **54%** report emotional stress
- **43%** experience mental health concerns
- **24%** feel like they don't belong[2]

Now imagine standing in Joshua's shoes. He had once spied out the land and seen with his own eyes the towering descendants of Anak, giants in the land. In comparison, the Israelites felt like grasshoppers. Yet, God told Joshua to rise, cross the Jordan, and take the land.

And Joshua wasn't just facing giants. He was **stepping into Moses's shoes.** Deuteronomy 34:10–12 says, "There has not arisen a prophet since in Israel like Moses . . . for all the signs and wonders . . . for all the mighty power and all the great deeds." Taking over from a leader of that stature must have been overwhelming.

To make things even harder, the **Jordan River was at flood stage**. Crossing it wasn't just inconvenient. It was dangerous. From a human perspective, the timing was all wrong.

But Joshua moved forward anyway. He held on to God's promises and responded with strong and courageous faith.

In Deuteronomy 31:8, Moses told him, "It is the Lord who goes before you. He will be with you; He will not leave you or forsake you. Do not fear or be dismayed."

Later, in Deuteronomy 31:23, the Lord Himself commissioned Joshua, "Be strong and courageous, for you shall bring the people of Israel into the land that I swore to give them. I will be with you."

And in Joshua 1, we see those promises reaffirmed again and again.

You might think, "That's great for Joshua, but what about me?" Here's the good news: As New Testament believers, we have the Holy Spirit living within us. We are never alone. Jesus Himself promised in Matthew 28:20, "I am with you always, to the end of the age."

And Hebrews 13:5–6 reminds us, "'I will never leave you nor forsake you.' So we can confidently say, 'The Lord is my helper; I will not fear; what can man do to me?'"

When we truly know that God is with us, we can face our challenges with boldness. Scripture encourages us to cast our cares on the Lord, to bring our fears and anxieties to Him, and to trust that the peace of God, which surpasses all understanding, will guard our hearts and minds in Christ Jesus.

Rest in His promises.
Trust in His presence.

So today, whatever is weighing on you—whatever you're afraid of—take a moment to tell your heavenly Father. Rest in His promises. Trust in His presence. **The Lord will be with you.**

COURAGEOUS STEP:

Fear. Anxiety. Despair. Learn to recognize when they begin to rise up within you. Immediately, take a few moments and talk to God about it, just like you were talking to a counselor or a friend. Acknowledge your fear, and ask God to make His presence known to you. Pursue a calm yet confident trust in God to quiet the voice of fear, anxiety, and despair.

Do Not Be Frightened or Dismayed

Joshua 1:9: "Have I not commanded you? Be strong and courageous. Do not be frightened, and do not be dismayed, for the Lord your God is with you wherever you go."

Joshua 8:1: "And the Lord said to Joshua, 'Do not fear and do not be dismayed. Take all the fighting men with you, and arise, go up to Ai. See, I have given into your hand the king of Ai, and his people, his city, and his land.'"

Joshua 10:8: "And the Lord said to Joshua, 'Do not fear them, for I have given them into your hands. Not a man of them shall stand before you.'"

The Lord repeatedly commanded Joshua to be strong and courageous. But He didn't stop there. God also told him what not to do: *"Do not be frightened. Do not be dismayed."* These commands are restated throughout the book of Joshua. God was shaping Joshua's mindset by replacing fear with faith, anxiety with confidence, and panic with peace.

In our modern context, we might phrase it like this: **do not be anxious.** So, let's keep journeying forward in this discussion.

Books like *The Anxious Generation: How the Great Rewiring of Childhood Is Causing an Epidemic of Mental Health* speak to what many of us already feel: an explosion of anxiety in our culture. As someone who lives and serves on a college campus, I hear it constantly. Students are anxious about assignments, tests, internships, jobs, relationships, and social belonging.

Let's be clear: I'm not denying the reality of clinical anxiety or its medical roots for some people. But we can still say that fear and anxiety are common emotional struggles and ones that the Bible does not ignore. In Joshua's case, God's answer wasn't a removal of difficult circumstances; it was a reminder of His presence and promises.

We've already seen that we can overcome fear and dismay **because God is with us**. But let's add a few more foundational truths:

- God knows the future.
- God will one day make all things new.
- This world is not our eternal home; we will live again.
- God is sovereign over all things.
- He directs the hearts of rulers like streams of water (Prov. 21:1).
- He cares for us more than sparrows or lilies (Matt. 6:26–29).

If these things are true, and they are, then the right response is to trust God.

Often, our anxiety stems from focusing too much on ourselves or our circumstances. We feel the weight of control and responsibility that only God was meant to carry. At other times, we're too fixated on the temporal rather than the eternal. But when we fix our eyes on God's promises, we find peace.

Philippians 4:6–7 encourages us, "Do not be anxious about anything, but in everything by prayer and supplication with thanksgiving let your requests be made known to God. And the peace of God, which surpasses all understanding, will guard your hearts and your minds in Christ Jesus."

Our last courageous action was: **when fear, anxiety, or despair rise up, talk to your heavenly Father in prayer.** Now, let's go one step farther. Name what's troubling you. Speak the truth of scripture to yourself and replace the lies that the enemy uses to enslave us.

Build your foundation through:

- Daily reading of scripture
- Persistent prayer
- Involvement in a local church
- A personal walk with God

As you do these things, you will grow in strong and courageous faith, but it takes time. The more we behold Jesus, the more the Spirit transforms us to be like Him. Stated another way, **we keep looking to Christ until we look like Christ.**

So, friends, *don't be anxious! God's got this!* Do not be frightened or dismayed. Respond with **strong and courageous faith** rooted in the unshakable truth of God's Word.

> ### COURAGEOUS STEP:
> Speak truth to yourself. Replace the lies of the enemy with the truth of scripture. The enemy wants to keep you afraid and inactive. The truth of scripture is that God controls all and uses us to do amazing things for His glory.

The Faith of Rahab

Joshua 2:11b: "The Lord your God, he is God in the heavens above and on the earth beneath."

Two spies enter a foreign land. Maybe they decide the safest place to hide is in a kind of public lodging—a place where strangers come and go without raising too many questions. A house built into the city wall. A house run by a woman named Rahab... Rahab the harlot. A place where they practice the oldest profession in the world.

Why is she there? Was she abandoned by her husband? Did he die? Did she never marry? Was this her only option? Had life pushed her into survival mode, forcing her to sell herself just to stay alive? We don't know the details. But we do know what happens next.

These spies are no James Bond or Jason Bourne. They're discovered almost immediately. The king of Jericho sends orders to arrest them. And then, the unthinkable: Rahab commits treason. She hides the men on her roof under stalks of flax and sends the king's agents on a wild goose chase outside the city gates. She lies. She deceives her government. She risks her life for two strangers. Why?

Because Rahab has heard things.

Her house is full of travelers and rumors. And from those reports, she knows three things:

1. The Lord has given Israel the land.
2. Terror has fallen on Jericho.
3. The people are paralyzed. They have no courage left.

But how does she know this? She offers two key examples:

- The Lord dried up the waters of the Red Sea.
- Israel defeated Sihon and Og, two Amorite kings, and devoted them to destruction.

And did you notice something crucial? Rahab uses the **personal name of God: YHWH.** She doesn't attribute the Red Sea crossing to a natural disaster or freak weather event. No windstorm. No earthquake. No coincidence. *The Lord* dried up the sea. She acknowledges God's hand.

In this moment of crisis, Rahab responds with **strong and courageous faith**, just as Joshua was commanded to in chapter 1. She pleads with the spies to show her and her family "kindness," the Hebrew word *hesed*, often translated as steadfast love. It's the covenantal, loyal love that God shows to His people repeatedly throughout the Old Testament.

Rahab doesn't stop at belief. She acts. She lets the spies down through a window. She ties a scarlet cord in that window as a sign of her trust. She gathers her family. She keeps silent about the mission. Think of the courage this took, telling her family, *"I've committed treason and made a deal with our enemies."* They could have turned her in. She could have panicked and confessed. But she didn't.

Her strong and courageous faith reveals something deeper: **God was already at work.**

- He prepared a place for the spies to be hidden.
- He prepared Rahab's heart to believe.
- He caused Jericho's people to fear.

Rahab's name reappears in the New Testament as a model of faith.

The Lord not only saved Rahab, He redeemed her story. She married Salmon. They had a son named Boaz, who later married Ruth the Moabitess. From their family line came King David and, eventually, King Jesus.

Jesus had no issue including a prostitute in His family tree because Jesus came to save sinners. The story of Rahab reminds us: It's not about where you came from or what you've done. It's about having **strong and courageous faith** in the living God.

The truth is, we are all Rahab—broken people in need of salvation. And like Rahab, we must choose: will we trust in God's power and promises or in our own fading strength?

Pray today and ask the Lord to give you the faith of Rahab.

COURAGEOUS STEP:

What past mistake are you allowing to define your future? Write it down. Ask God to forgive you if you haven't already. Now that God has forgiven you as He promised He would, forgive yourself. You will have to do this more than once because we tend to pick back up the things we put down.

Did you write it down? Now, destroy that paper or delete that note. It's forgiven and not remembered. Stop looking in the rearview mirror and begin looking out the windshield at your future strong and courageous faith.

The Scarlet Thread of Redemption

Joshua 2:21b: "And she tied the scarlet cord in the window."

Where did the scarlet cord come from? Was it lying around? Did the spies bring it with them? Of all things, why would the sovereign Lord of the universe use a **scarlet cord** and ensure that specific detail was recorded in the book of Joshua?

This is no coincidence.

In order for Rahab and her family to be saved, the spies instructed her: "Tie this scarlet cord in the window through which you let us down, and you shall gather into your house your father and mother, your brothers, and all your father's household" (Joshua 2:18b).

Rahab responded with strong and courageous faith. She obeyed. She believed and lived.

Now, think back to Egypt. In Exodus, the blood of the Passover lamb had to be spread on the doorposts to spare the firstborn from death. This event became a defining moment in Israel's history—a celebration of God's deliverance.

The Israelites were commanded to keep the Passover as a statute forever, and even foreigners who joined Israel were required to observe it. The Passover became a tool to teach future generations about God's power to redeem. And what marked that moment? **Scarlet blood** was a symbol of salvation.

Now, fast forward to the New Testament. John the Baptist is baptizing sinners in the same Jordan River Israel crossed. When he sees Jesus, he declares, "Behold, the Lamb of God, who takes away the sin of the world!" (John 1:29b).

Why call Jesus the Lamb of God? Because the Passover lamb in Exodus was only a shadow pointing forward to the true, ultimate sacrifice. Just as the scarlet cord in Rahab's window pointed backward to Passover, it also pointed forward to the cross.

Rahab was not saved by a scarlet cord. She was saved through faith in the Lord. But her faith wasn't mere agreement with facts or passive belief. Scripture tells us even demons believe—and shudder (James 2:19). Rahab's faith was active. She took bold steps. She risked her life. She changed allegiances from the kingdom of Jericho to the Kingdom of God.

That's why James writes, "And in the same way was not also Rahab the prostitute justified by works when she received the messengers and sent them out by another way?" (James 2:25).

So, let me ask: are you trusting in a scarlet thread?

That might sound silly, but some of us are trusting in a **moment**, a **memory**, or a **religious ritual**. A prayer at summer camp. Walking an aisle. Baptism. A confirmation class. These things can be good, but they do not save.

Salvation comes when we believe in our heart and confess with our mouth that Jesus is Lord. When we repent of sin and change our allegiance from the kingdoms of this world to the Kingdom of God. We trust not in a scarlet thread but in the **scarlet blood of Jesus** shed on the cross to take away the sin of the world.

This same Jesus voluntarily laid down His life, rose from the grave three days later, and is coming again to make all things new.

If you look closely, you'll see it all throughout the Bible, little signs and symbols, scarlet threads woven through a magnificent tapestry, all pointing us to the cross. That cross where Jesus offers redemption for all mankind.

COURAGEOUS STEP:

Examine your own heart today. Are you trusting in the faith of your parents, a campfire decision, baptism, or some ritual rather than trusting in Jesus? Are you trying to work for God's favor? If so, stop! We are saved by grace alone through faith alone in Christ alone.

Right now, tell God how you feel, ask Him to forgive you of your sins and put your trust in Him. Then, stop trying to earn His favor and trust that God has declared you righteous and adopted you into His family.

No Water Too Deep or Too Wide

Joshua 3:13, 15b; 4:18b: "And when the soles of the feet of the priests bearing the ark of the Lord, the Lord of all the earth, shall rest in the waters of the Jordan, the waters of the Jordan shall be cut off from flowing, and the waters coming down from above shall stand in one heap . . . (now the Jordan overflows all its banks throughout the time of harvest) . . . The waters of the Jordan returned to their place and overflowed all its banks, as before."

The spring rains begin to fall. Snow from Mount Hermon melts and rushes into the Jordan River. A steep elevation drop causes the water to gain speed. During harvest season, the river overflows its banks. Brush on either side is swallowed by the rising water. The fords usually provided safe crossing points, but in harvest season, they become dangerous and impassable. The water is wide, deep, and wild.

Yet early in the morning, Joshua and all the people of Israel set out and came to the Jordan. There, they camped for three days.

You can imagine the tension. Mothers hear the roar of rushing water. A father glances nervously at his small children, ages seven, five, and three, wondering how they'll get across. Murmurs spread through the camp. Questions arise. *Who is this new leader? What is he thinking?*

Joshua, aware of the fear and doubt, gathers the people and says, "Come here and listen to the words of the Lord your God" (Joshua 3:9).

Then he makes a bold declaration, "Here is how you shall know that the living God is among you and that he will without fail drive out from before you the Canaanites, the Hittites, the Hivites, the Perizzites, the Girgashites, the Amorites, and the Jebusites" (Joshua 3:10).

Joshua proclaims that the God of Israel is living. He's not a dead idol carved from stone or wood. Yahweh, the Creator of the world, is present and active. Then Joshua calls his shot: as soon as the priests' feet touch the edge of the river while carrying the ark of the covenant, the waters will stop and pile up in a heap.

If he's wrong, he's finished as a leader.

Can you imagine the pressure? The sleepless nights? The murmuring from the crowd: *Why now? Why not wait for the floodwaters to subside? We've waited 40 years—what's a few more weeks? Joshua is being reckless. Someone needs to speak up before we all drown.*

But sometimes, God brings us to a point where we have no other option but to trust Him. Sometimes, the odds are stacked so heavily against us that we realize we cannot win in our own strength.

This was one of those moments.

And just as Joshua declared, the waters of the Jordan stopped 15 miles upstream and stood in a heap. The people crossed over **on dry ground**. And they crossed in haste. Can you blame them?

God orchestrated the flood-stage crossing to prove that **nothing is too hard for Him**. His purpose is made clear in Joshua 4:24, "So that all the peoples of the earth may know that the hand of the Lord is mighty, that you may fear the Lord your God forever."

Maybe today you're facing a flood of your own. Maybe your circumstances feel impossible.

Hand it over to God.

The crossing of the Jordan reminds us: **there is no river too deep or too wide for our God**. He is the Lord Almighty. He makes a way where there is no way.

So, like the Israelites, follow Him because "you have never been this way before" (Joshua 3:4). Step forward in faith. Trust Him with what's ahead.

No water is too deep. No river is too wide.

COURAGEOUS STEP:

Identify an obstacle that feels impossible. Surrender it to God in prayer, confirming that your request aligns with scripture and God's character. Take the next step forward in faith, trusting Him to make a way.

On Dry Ground

Joshua 3:17: "Now the priests bearing the ark of the covenant of the Lord stood firmly on dry ground in the midst of the Jordan, and all Israel was passing over on dry ground until all the nation finished passing over the Jordan."

Have you ever considered the biblical authors' fascination with **dry ground**?

Repetition in scripture often signals something significant. In this one verse, the author mentions twice that the people and priests crossed the river on *dry ground*. That's no accident. We know from the chapter that the Jordan was in flood stage and had overflowed its banks. Under normal conditions, the riverbed would be muddy or slick. But the text goes out of its way to highlight that it was dry.

I remember playing and fishing in a local river as a boy. When the water rose over the banks, the edges turned soft and muddy. Even when a summer drought caused the water to recede, the rocks in the riverbed were slippery. Anyone who has tried to walk in a river knows that *standing firmly* is not the norm.

We can't say definitively why the author emphasized this detail, but Moses made the same point in Exodus 14:22 at the Red Sea: "The people of Israel went into the midst of the sea on dry ground." This crossing of the Jordan paralleled the Red Sea crossing for the previous generation (see Joshua 4:24). It was a tangible reminder that God, and not nature, was in control.

Perhaps some ancient skeptics tried to explain away the miracle. Maybe they said a wind blew from both directions or a landslide blocked the water upstream. But then someone would respond: **"But they walked across on dry ground."**

This detail testifies to the miraculous. The same God who spoke the world into existence now commands His creation to obey. God parted the Red Sea. God halted the Jordan. Jesus stilled the storm. And the wind, the waves, the rivers, and even the ground itself *obeyed Him*.

Israel needed to be reminded of God's power. They needed to know that the same God who delivered them from Egypt would now give them the Promised Land. That **no wall**—not even the walls of Jericho—could stop Him. That **no army** could withstand His heavenly hailstones. That **no cosmic order** could resist His will, not even the sun in the sky.

They needed to know and so do we.

Our God is all-powerful and all-knowing! The authors recorded these events for *our* benefit. Whatever you're facing today, or will face tomorrow, know this: **dry ground awaits**. God is able. You can trust Him to provide a way forward.

He's powerful enough to do it and faithful enough to see it through.

One day, Jesus would come to Earth to bear the penalty of our sin. When His work on the cross was complete, the skies grew dark, the earth quaked, and the veil in the temple was torn from top to bottom. Then, three days later, Jesus conquered death. The stone covering the opening of the tomb obeyed the voice of God and rolled away. And the Savior of the world walked out on dry ground.

COURAGEOUS STEP:

What is your favorite miracle? God turns the impossible into the possible. Think about how powerful your God is and all of the miracles He has accomplished. Be amazed at God's Creation. Praise Him for His good works and take joy in the fact that our God reigns.

Twelve Stones

Joshua 4:21–22a: "And he said to the people of Israel, 'When your children ask their fathers in times to come, "What do these stones mean?" then you shall let your children know.'"

Twelve stones.

The Lord gave clear instructions, and Joshua followed them. Twelve men, one from each tribe, were chosen to take a stone from the middle of the Jordan River. They carried those stones about eight miles to Gilgal, where Joshua set up a **memorial** to God's power and faithfulness.

Twice in Joshua 4, we read the phrase: "When your children ask in times to come, 'What do these stones mean?'" (verses 6 and 21). Why? Because the Bible understands something deeply true about the human condition: **forgetfulness erodes faith**.

These twelve stones were meant to serve as lasting reminders:

- God dried up the waters of the Jordan before His people.

- God had once done the same at the Red Sea.
- Together, these miracles declare that the Lord alone is all-powerful and that the proper response is reverent, faithful obedience.

But here's the problem: We forget. All of us do.

God proves Himself faithful in a time of great need. Then life gets better. We get comfortable. Maybe even complacent. When another trial comes, we doubt. We forget that God has already shown Himself trustworthy again and again.

That's why we need twelve stones.

Every word God has promised will come to pass. He will be with us. And when God does something extraordinary in our lives, we should commemorate it. We need our own stones of remembrance, personal markers that remind us of His faithfulness.

Maybe it's a jar of written prayer requests and answered prayers, a bracelet, a journal, or a simple decoration in your home. Whatever it is, let it serve as a tangible reminder of what God has done, something you can look to during seasons of struggle or doubt.

Why? Because these moments of divine intervention aren't everyday events. They are unusual and, by their nature, easily forgotten if not recorded.

Maybe you haven't had that moment yet. It will come. But even now, God in His wisdom has recorded these moments for *you* in His Word. The book of Joshua stands as a memorial to God's faithfulness and a testimony that He sees, acts, and keeps His promises. So even if you don't yet have a personal story, you have scripture. And that is more than enough to start.

Read your Bible. Memorize scripture. Fill your heart and mind with reminders that **God is faithful. We can trust Him.**

And when that moment comes, when God does something remarkable in your life or in your family's lives, go find your twelve stones. Set up a memorial. Tell the story. Proclaim that the Lord is almighty.

God is faithful. We can trust Him.

Because forgetfulness erodes faith. But remembrance strengthens it.

So build your memorial. Keep trusting God. And follow Him as He leads you toward the Promised Land to come.

COURAGEOUS STEP:

Doubt. It arises repeatedly. We doubt God. Today, choose a way to remember God's faithfulness. A jar where you store answered prayers on slips of paper. A note on your phone with a bullet point list of when God acted. A bracelet commemorating a major God moment in your lives. Develop a testimony of God's faithfulness to look back upon when you doubt and to share with future generations.

The Lord Exalts

Joshua 3:7: "The Lord said to Joshua, 'Today I will begin to exalt you in the sight of all Israel, that they may know that, as I was with Moses, so I will be with you.'"

Joshua 4:14: "On that day the Lord exalted Joshua in the sight of all Israel, and they stood in awe of him just as they had stood in awe of Moses, all the days of his life."

Have you ever wanted to be in charge? Maybe you've longed to lead, to have others admire your leadership, or to be seen as competent and respected.

So, what do we do? We work hard. We grow frustrated when we're overlooked. Sometimes, we even compare ourselves to others, justifying our readiness to lead.

But notice how Joshua was exalted. Not through self-promotion. Not through clever maneuvering. **God exalted him,** in His time, not Joshua's.

Joshua served. He was Moses's assistant. He led in battle without leading the people. He was one of the faithful spies who gave a courageous report. And then—**when God was ready**—He said, "Today I will begin to exalt you."

But that moment didn't come without pressure.

Israel was camped beside the flooded Jordan River. The sound of rushing water filled the air. The banks had overflowed. The terrain was dangerous. Joshua stood before the people with God's command in hand, and surely he must have thought, "Lord, if You don't come through, I'm finished."

Yet Joshua wasn't called to part the river or dry the ground. Joshua was called to be faithful.

And God did come through. The Jordan stood still. The ground turned dry. The people crossed safely.

And on that day, "the Lord exalted Joshua in the sight of all Israel." They stood in awe of him, just as they had of Moses.

So what's the lesson for those of us who long to lead?

God exalts.

God is the one who grants favor.
God is the one who moves hearts.
God is the one who opens doors and closes them.

And our calling? To serve faithfully, not ambitiously. To desire leadership, not for praise or position, but for the purpose of serving others and glorifying God.

In the Kingdom of God, "if anyone would be first, he must be last of all and servant of all" (Mark 9:35). If you only want a title, you're not ready. If you only want praise but not the work, you're missing the point. But if you're content to serve quietly and wait patiently, then maybe. And if God does choose to exalt you, make sure you point all the glory back to Him.

Because at the end of the day, you didn't do anything that extraordinary. Yes, you served wisely and faithfully, but God is the one who controls outcomes. He humbles and exalts. He opens and closes. He leads and appoints.

So here are your questions for today:

- Do I trust God enough to give Him my future?
- Do I trust Him enough to serve faithfully, even if no one notices?
- Am I content to serve whether or not He ever exalts me?

That's the kind of heart God delights to exalt.

COURAGEOUS STEP:

Seek to serve without recognition. Do something nice for someone else without letting anyone know. Write an encouraging note. Clean up a mess. Pick up trash on the ground. Do something just because it is good and right without telling anyone. God knows, and that is who we serve.

Fear of the Lord

Joshua 4:24: "So that all the peoples of the earth may know that the hand of the Lord is mighty, that you may fear the Lord your God forever."

Why did God dry up the Red Sea and cause the waters of the Jordan River to stand still?

So that the world would know the Lord is mighty—and that we would fear Him.

These miraculous displays weren't for spectacle. God wasn't showing off. He revealed His power for two distinct purposes:

1. To inspire fear in those who serve Him.

Let's be honest: Many of us flinch at the word *fear*. It sounds negative. But scripture paints a different picture. Proverbs 9:10 tells us that "the fear of the Lord is the beginning of wisdom."

To fear the Lord means we understand that He is all-powerful, sovereign, and holy, and we are not. It's not about fearing

God as if He's cruel or unpredictable. Rather, it's a reverential awe of His greatness, goodness, and authority. It's the deep respect a child has for a wise and loving father, combined with an awareness that stepping outside His boundaries leads to discipline.

God is my heavenly Father who delights to give good gifts to His children. But He is also just. He brings correction and judgment when we rebel. Healthy fear includes both awe of His mercy and respect for His holiness.

Do you fear the Lord?

- Do you grasp how mighty He truly is?
- Do you realize He could undo all your plans or possessions with a single word?
- Do you understand how small we are in this vast universe He created?

We are a mist, a vapor, a blade of grass. Here today, gone tomorrow. Yet God is eternal. He is the same yesterday, today, and forever. He spoke the stars into place. He holds the universe together by the word of His power. It is *wise* and *healthy* to reflect on our smallness and His greatness.

2. To bring *terror* to those who reject Him.

Those who refuse to fear the Lord rightly now will one day face Him in terror.

To reject God is to reject His offer of forgiveness by grace alone through faith alone. It is to choose to pay the penalty for your sin yourself, to live in willful rebellion, and to face the justice of a holy God without a mediator.

This is exactly what we see in Joshua 5:1. The kings of the Amorites and Canaanites, once proud and powerful, heard what God had done, and "their hearts melted." They had no strength left, no will to resist. After centuries of rebellion, judgment had come. They realized they were powerless against Israel's God.

One day, that will be true for everyone who rejects Christ. "It is appointed for man to die once, and after that comes judgment" (Hebrews 9:27).

But here's the good news:

For those who fear the Lord **now**, there is **no fear** of judgment.

We are covered in Christ's righteousness.
We belong to Him.
We await His return with hope, not dread.

But for those who refuse to bow now, the day is coming when they will. "Every knee should bow ... and every tongue confess that Jesus Christ is Lord, to the glory of God the Father" (Philippians 2:10–11).

So let's **fear the Lord now**—with reverence, humility, and joyful obedience—**so we don't have to be terrified of Him later.**

COURAGEOUS STEP:

Today, worship the Lord. Choose your favorite worship song and sing it directly to God, praising Him. Pray to God, thanking Him for His character without asking God for anything . . . no requests, just praise. Read your favorite verse and thank God for including it in scripture. God is good and worthy of our worship.

Time to Obey

Joshua 5:6: "For the people of Israel walked forty years in the wilderness, until all the nation, the men of war who came out of Egypt, perished, because they did not obey the voice of the Lord; the Lord swore to them that he would not let them see the land that the Lord had sworn to their fathers to give to us, a land flowing with milk and honey."

We know the story. Israel disobeyed.

Twelve spies were sent into the Promised Land. Ten returned with fear-filled reports. Only Joshua and Caleb trusted God, and only they entered the land.

This passage reminds us of the **consequences of disobedience**, but it also teaches us something deeper: **obedience must come before blessing**.

God had given a command to Abraham in Genesis 17:12: every male was to be circumcised on the eighth day. This wasn't optional. It was a covenant sign. God even warned in Genesis 17:14, "Any uncircumcised male . . . shall be cut off from his people; he has broken my covenant."

But Israel had been disobedient.
They had neglected this command.
Before they could experience God's victory and blessing, they needed to obey.

Picture the scene: The Jordan River has miraculously stopped. The people cross over on dry ground. Spirits are high. Momentum is on their side. From a human standpoint, now is the time to march forward and strike. But instead, Joshua gives a command from the Lord to take flint knives and circumcise all the men.

From a military perspective, this seems foolish. They're vulnerable. Their backs are to a flooded river. Any attack would be devastating. Surely, this should have been done *before* they crossed, not now. Was this a leadership failure?

No; it was a test of faith.

God was teaching His people to trust Him completely, even when it didn't make sense. They had to obey first, and then He would protect and bless them.

Not only had they neglected circumcision in the wilderness, but they had also failed to keep the Passover. Both were critical acts of worship and remembrance. Now, as they stood on the threshold of promise, it was time to repent, not just with words but with action.

They had to obey.

Sometimes we find ourselves in difficult circumstances because we've chosen to disobey God. We think we know better. We seek immediate gratification. We pursue worldly pleasures. We find it hard to trust a God we cannot see. So, we do things our way.

But like Eve in the garden, we eventually discover something: The Devil lied. God's way *is* best. Obedience leads to blessing. Disobedience brings consequences.

Do you want true peace, joy, and contentment? Do you want your life to flourish under God's favor?

Then trust and obey. For, as the old hymn, "Trust and Obey," reminds us, "There's no other way to be happy in Jesus, but to trust and obey."

So, where are you today? Are there areas where you're delaying obedience, waiting until it's more convenient?

Let me encourage you—**it's time to obey**.

COURAGEOUS STEP:

Identify and write down one area where delayed obedience has crept into your life. Take the first step toward full obedience. Depending on the issue, you may need to tell someone about your struggle, seek counseling, develop a long-term plan for growth, talk to your pastor, or get help. Today, exercise your faith muscle by courageously taking a step towards full obedience.

No More Manna

Joshua 5:11–12: "And the day after the Passover, on that very day, they ate of the produce of the land, unleavened cakes and parched grain. And the manna ceased the day after they ate of the produce of the land. And there was no longer manna for the people of Israel, but they ate of the fruit of the land of Canaan that year."

God provides.

But He doesn't always provide in the same way. And far too often, we take His provision for granted.

For 40 years, **God provided manna** to the people of Israel. They wandered in the wilderness, dependent on Him for food and water. At times, they grumbled, but the manna faithfully sustained their lives daily.

Then they crossed the Jordan.
They obeyed.
They consecrated themselves.
They circumcised their sons.
They celebrated the Passover.

And then, on that very day, they finally tasted the produce of the Promised Land.

God fulfills His promises. Can you imagine that first bite? Like someone finishing a restricted diet or recovering from a medical procedure, you take that first taste of something fresh and flavorful. Sweet, satisfying, and so welcome. A reminder that God fulfills His promises.

But scripture points out something profound:

The manna ceased.

The very next day, it was gone. God no longer provided food from heaven. Now, the people would eat from the land itself. I wonder if anyone complained. *Manna was so easy. I just picked it up from the ground. Now, I have to farm? To work?*

God still provided, but in a different way. And I'm sure someone felt entitled to the old way or wished they could have both.

The same thing often happens to us.

In my life, God has provided in many different ways:

- Through my parents when I was young.
- Through a small business that met my needs.
- Through subsidized housing during our early years of marriage.

- Through a job that covered tuition and steady employment.
- Through a generous relative who unexpectedly helped us buy our first house and support an adoption.
- And later, through the opportunity to serve, the health to work, and the income to be generous to others.

God's provision has **never stopped,** but it has changed.

Can you see God's hand of provision in your own life? Have you paused to thank Him for His mercy and care? Or have you started to feel entitled to His provision?

That sense of entitlement is a warning sign. It's the root of greed and jealousy. But God calls us to gratitude and generosity. As we grow, we are also invited to become part of God's provision in the lives of others.

Life comes in seasons. Sometimes, we **receive manna.** Sometimes, we **reap the fruit of the land.** And sometimes, God calls us to **share the manna**—to become a means of provision for someone else.

So wherever you are today, choose to be grateful even if there's *no more manna* because the Provider hasn't changed.

COURAGEOUS STEP:

Pause for a moment and thank God for His provision in the past and the present. Embrace where God has you and look for ways to express gratitude for the blessings in your life, satisfaction with what God has given you, and faithful stewardship of what God has entrusted to you.

Sword Drawn: Are You on God's Side?

Joshua 5:13–15: "When Joshua was by Jericho, he lifted up his eyes and looked, and behold, a man was standing before him with his drawn sword in his hand. And Joshua went to him and said to him, 'Are you for us, or for our adversaries?' And he said, 'No; but I am the commander of the army of the Lord. Now I have come.' And Joshua fell on his face to the earth and worshiped and said to him, 'What does my Lord say to his servant?' And the commander of the Lord's army said to Joshua, 'Take off your sandals from your feet, for the place where you are standing is holy.' And Joshua did so."

Can you imagine the scene?

The Israelites had just been circumcised. The men were recovering. Joshua, already circumcised long before, walked near Jericho, perhaps as a general surveying the challenge ahead. He knew the task. A nomadic people would now need to conquer a fortified, walled city without siege equipment, towers, or battering rams. Maybe he was deep in thought, anxious about what lay ahead.

And then he looked up.

A man stood before him, sword drawn. Ready for battle. Joshua doesn't flee. He doesn't call for reinforcements. Instead, in a moment of **strong and courageous faith**, he steps forward and asks the man, "Are you for us, or for our adversaries?" A fair question—was this a friend, a foe, or a fight?

But the answer is startling: **"No."**

That wasn't one of the options.

Then came the revealing statement: "I am the commander of the army of the Lord. Now I have come." Don't miss this: **the Lord wasn't on Joshua's side.**

Wait, didn't God fight for Israel? Yes, but only when Israel was on God's side. That's the key. The real question isn't: "Is God on our side?" The question is: **"Are we on His?"**

God is not obligated to fight battles that we choose in pride or presumption. But He will fight every battle that aligns with His purposes, His Word, and His glory. Our task is not to recruit God to our cause but to submit ourselves to His.

I believe this was a theophany, an appearance of God in the Old Testament. Possibly a Christophany, a pre-incarnate appearance of Christ. Why? Because Joshua worships, and the figure receives it. Angels never accept worship. They always point glory back to God. But here, as with Jesus in the New Testament, this commander accepts Joshua's adoration.

Joshua then asks the right question: "What does my Lord say to His servant?" The response? "Take off your sandals from your feet, for the place where you are standing is holy."

Why was it holy? **Because the Lord was there.**

It's a clear echo of the burning bush, when Moses met God and was told the same thing (Exodus 3:5).

What lessons can we draw from this sacred encounter?

1. **God is holy.** He is not like us. He is above us—utterly pure, utterly powerful, and utterly sovereign.
2. **God is not here to serve our agenda.** He doesn't exist to grant our wishes like a divine genie. Our prayers shouldn't be a Christmas list. We should come before Him asking, "What does my Lord say to His servant?"
3. **We are called to service, worship, and obedience.** God doesn't need us, but He invites us to join Him. Not as equals, but as servants under His command.
4. **We must choose whose side we're on.** The sword is drawn. The King is present. You cannot remain neutral. You are either surrendering or resisting.

So, the question remains: **are you on God's side?**

Will you bow in reverence like Joshua? Or will you keep demanding that God fight for your personal battles, your ambitions, and your plans?

There are only two responses:

- Turn from sin and worship the King.
- Continue in rebellion and face the eternal consequences.

The sword is drawn. It's time to decide.

> **COURAGEOUS STEP:**
>
> Examine your heart. Be honest with yourself. Are you inviting God to join your team and accomplish your plans and desires? Are you seeking to join God's team, surrendering your agenda and seeking His will? You must seek to serve God for His glory, knowing that ultimately it will result in your joy.

The Best-Laid Plans

Joshua 6:3–5: "You shall march around the city, all the men of war going around the city once. Thus shall you do for six days. Seven priests shall bear seven trumpets of rams' horns before the ark. On the seventh day you shall march around the city seven times, and the priests shall blow the trumpets. And when they make a long blast with the ram's horn, when you hear the sound of the trumpet, then all the people shall shout with a great shout, and the wall of the city will fall down flat, and the people shall go up, everyone straight before him."

The author tells us that Jericho was tightly shut up. No one going in, no one coming out. Then the Lord tells Joshua, "See, I have given Jericho into your hand" (Joshua 6:2). But from a human standpoint, that didn't seem remotely true. The king and his warriors rested safely behind thick, fortified walls. Archaeologists speculate that Jericho had double walls with living quarters in between, nearly impenetrable.

Yes, we know from Rahab that their hearts had melted in fear. But I wonder if some in Jericho still trusted the walls more than they feared the God of Israel? Did they think,

"They might want to fight us, but they'll never breach these defenses"? Maybe some Israelites thought the same. "These walls are massive. How will we ever get in?"

But **God had a plan.**

And let's be honest: it didn't make sense.

March around the walls once a day for six days. Then, on the seventh day, march around seven times. Have the priests blow their trumpets. Have the people shout. And then the walls would fall.

Let's be even more honest: This plan makes zero sense from a human perspective. Marching won't shake the ground. Trumpets and shouting don't topple stone walls. The people inside Jericho likely laughed. They probably thought the Israelites were crazy. But God had commanded Israel to remain silent, no responding, no debating, just trust and obey.

This scene makes me think of marriage in our culture today.

God's Word is clear: A man and a woman are to leave their families and become one flesh. Sex is reserved for marriage. Yet the world mocks that vision. In today's culture, promiscuity is praised. "Body count" is discussed with pride. Entertainment glorifies sex without covenant and pleasure without responsibility. People are viewed not as image-bearers but as objects.

But let's look at the results. God's design, though mocked, would virtually eliminate STDs. It would reduce unplanned pregnancies and fatherlessness. It would provide children with stable homes led by both a mother and a father, which studies confirm is still the most effective, stable, and healthy family structure.

So, what do we do when God's plan doesn't make sense to the world?

We obey it anyway.

Israel obeyed God's strange plan. They marched. They blew the trumpets. They shouted. And then, God acted.

Can you imagine the noise? The rumbling ground. Dust clouding the air. Eyes stinging, mouths dry, hands shielding their faces. Then silence. And when the dust settled . . . the walls were gone.

All except one section: the place where the scarlet thread hung. God destroyed the city, but He saved Rahab and her family—those who believed.

In that moment, God revealed both His mercy and His justice.

One day, God will again show both fully. He will complete salvation for those who trust Him. And He will bring judgment to those who reject Him.

So here's the question: **whose plan will you follow?**

Will you trust your best-laid plans? Will you follow the world's wisdom? Or will you trust God's plan, given clearly in His Word?

The best plan has already been laid out for us in scripture. And the wise will do what Israel did: trust and obey.

> **COURAGEOUS STEP:**
>
> Have you bought into the lies of the world? This possession will make you happy, this action will make you popular, or this sin will provide lasting satisfaction. Do you trust God's plan and God's way? You must examine your thinking, realizing that the Bible provides these stories for your spiritual growth. God's way is best. You must trust and follow His plan.

Devoted Things

Joshua 6:18: "But you, keep yourselves from the things devoted to destruction, lest when you have devoted them you take any of the devoted things and make the camp of Israel a thing for destruction and bring trouble upon it."

God warned them . . . **"Keep yourselves from the things devoted to destruction."**

The command was clear. So was the consequence: If you take them, you "make the camp of Israel a thing for destruction and bring trouble upon it."

The warning is repeated in Joshua 7. Yet despite its clarity, **Achan** disobeyed.

This is the nature of temptation. It's subtle at first. It grows. And if we don't confront it early, it consumes.

We'll explore the consequences in a later devotion, but today we focus on the command itself and the way it was violated. Understanding how Achan fell may help us stand firm when we face temptation.

When confronted, Achan confesses, "I saw among the spoil a beautiful cloak from Shinar, and 200 shekels of silver, and a bar of gold weighing 50 shekels" (Joshua 7:21).

First, he **saw** items of beauty and value.

Then, he **coveted** them. To covet means to yearn to possess something. Achan lingered in his look.

Finally, **desire** took root. He likely began justifying the act in his mind. "It's just one cloak. Just a little silver. Just a bit of gold."

Rather than fleeing like Joseph did from Potiphar's wife, Achan **lingered**. He fed the desire, and it finally overtook him like the cresting of a wave. Sudden. Crashing. Devastating. Then, finally, "he took them" (Joshua 7:21).

After that, he **hid** them.

And sin, once hidden, rarely stays private. Whether others were complicit or unaware, Achan's sin eventually brought judgment on the entire community.

What does this mean for us?

God has given us clear commands too.

- "Whatever one sows, that will he also reap" (Galatians 6:7).
- "Be sure your sin will find you out" (Numbers 32:23).

- "Nothing is hidden that will not be made manifest" (Luke 8:17).

God sees everything. He even knows our thoughts. So what do we do when temptation appears?

We have a choice:

- We can linger, covet, and eventually sin.
- We can flee early.

We can look away, not linger. We can confess temptation to trusted friends or mentors. We can pray and ask the Spirit to help us resist. We can actively seek the way of escape that God promises (1 Corinthians 10:13).

But if we delay too long, temptation becomes harder to resist. Sudden. Crashing. Devastating.

Not all sin brings immediate destruction, but it always brings damage. As God said to Israel in Joshua 7:13, "There are devoted things in your midst, O Israel. You cannot stand before your enemies until you take away the devoted things from among you."

Might this be true of us, too?

Do we lack victory in our Christian walk because we harbor hidden sin?
Have we tolerated what God has forbidden?
Have we made peace with what He's called us to destroy?

Maybe we, like Achan, have seen, coveted, and taken—and now wonder why we can't stand firm.

If so, the path is clear: Repent. Remove the devoted things. Return to obedience.

And by God's grace, we will stand again.

> **COURAGEOUS STEP:**
>
> Take a few moments in prayer. Ask God to reveal any hidden sin in your life. Confess it, repent of it, and remove anything that hinders your relationship with Him. Recognize that this hidden sin likely increases the fear, anxiety, and despair in your life, so remove it.

A Curse Fulfilled

Joshua 6:26: "Joshua laid an oath on them at that time, saying, 'Cursed before the Lord be the man who rises up and rebuilds this city, Jericho.

> "'At the cost of his firstborn shall he
> lay its foundation,
> and at the cost of his youngest son
> shall he set up its gates.'"

At first glance, it seems like an odd and out-of-place statement. After the miraculous fall of Jericho, Joshua issues a curse: anyone who rebuilds this city will do so at the cost of their firstborn and their youngest child.

It's a chilling pronouncement, and it's recorded in scripture for a reason.

Fast forward **over 500 years**, and we see the fulfillment:

"In his days Hiel of Bethel built Jericho. He laid its foundation at the cost of Abiram his firstborn, and set up its gates at the cost of his youngest son Segub, according to the word of the Lord, which He spoke by Joshua the son of Nun" (1 Kings 16:34).

Hiel rebuilt Jericho—and suffered the exact consequence Joshua foretold. Did he know about the curse? Did he disregard it? Or did he simply not believe God would actually follow through?

Whatever the case, one truth is clear: **God keeps His word.**
Even after centuries.
Even when culture forgets.
Even when no one else is paying attention.

So, let me ask you: Who do you trust? Do you truly believe scripture? Do you really believe God created the world, sent His Son Jesus to redeem us, forgives us by grace through faith, and is coming again to judge the wicked and make all things new?

I do. Not just because I've read it, but because I've seen it. I've studied scripture and lived long enough to see that God keeps His word every time.

And I've also lived long enough to see the shifting sands of culture, opinion, trends, and public morality. The world changes. But God does not.

You can't trust society, social media, or the so-called "wisdom" of influencers. The devil is the father of lies, and he wants to destroy you.

But **Jesus is the Way, the Truth, and the Life.**

If I could write a paragraph persuasive enough to cause you to trust God and His Word, I would. But my deeper prayer is this: that you'll open your eyes to the evidence found in the book of Joshua and all of scripture:

- God granted the Promised Land.
- God judged rebellion.
- **God fulfilled every promise.**
- God will keep every word He has spoken to us in scripture.

If you choose to trust God and build your life on the rock, you will stand against the storms of this world. But if you choose to build on sand, don't be surprised when the storm comes and everything collapses.

Because God keeps His promises. And if you rebel against Him, you may very well find, like Hiel, that **He fulfills His curses, too.**

COURAGEOUS STEP:

Today, you focus on God's punishment. Scripture tells us we will reap what we sow. There is judgment coming. Acknowledge where you are ignoring the warnings of scripture. Ask God to help you. You may not be ready yet. The Christian life is about progress and not perfection, so take the next step, even if that is admitting that you love your sin more than you love God.

Get UP!

Joshua 7:10–11a: "The Lord said to Joshua, 'Get up! Why have you fallen on your face? Israel has sinned.'"

I blew it.

I remember the thoughts running through my mind: *It's over. The Lord will never use me again. How could someone this foolish serve God and lead others to Him?*

The anxiety. The desperation. The shame.

I made a foolish leadership decision, naively, even with good intentions, but it cost dearly. It affected the organization I served and my family. I'll never forget the moment I collapsed in my driveway, face down, crying out to the Lord.

Joshua knew that kind of weight. His crisis wasn't due to his own sin but the sin of Achan. Yet as Israel's leader, Joshua bore the burden of their defeat at Ai. How do we know that? He was **on his face before the Lord**, crying out in despair.

And how did God respond?
"Get up!"
Israel has sinned.

What does this mean for us?

When we sin or make foolish choices, we must repent. We must be broken over our mistakes. We may walk through real consequences. But here's the key: **we cannot stay face down forever**.

Our God is merciful. He is slow to anger, rich in love, and full of grace. So when we cry out, when we confess, when we long to change—He hears us. And once we've dealt with the sin, **it's time to get up and move forward**.

Think of the Christian life like a long hike up a mountain.

- Sometimes the path is slow and winding.
- Sometimes we must navigate around hard obstacles.
- And sometimes ... we fall.

But when we fall, we don't quit the hike. We get up. We dust ourselves off. And we keep climbing, one slow step after another, in the same direction.

And we don't hike alone.

In the best-case scenario, we journey with other friends who encourage, support, challenge, and restore. When we fall, they help us up. When they fall, we do the same for them.

That's the beauty of the body of Christ.

So, yes, do all you can to guard your life. Stay in the Word. Pray for strength from the Spirit. Commit to a healthy church. Find a real Christian community. Pursue accountability. Build those spiritual muscles.

But know this: **even with your best efforts, you will fail.**

You'll wrestle with the flesh just like Paul in Romans 7:15: "I do not do what I want, but I do the very thing I hate." This war will rage until we go home to be with Jesus.

What do you do when you mess up? **Get up.** Repent. And keep going.

After the sin was dealt with, how did God speak to Joshua? He said, "Do not fear and do not be dismayed" (Joshua 8:1). He promised victory. Joshua's ministry wasn't over. Israel wasn't doomed. They had experienced a setback, but now it was time to get back to work.

And so must we.

Whatever mistake you've made, whatever burden you're carrying, if you've brought it to the Lord, **get up**. The world is broken. Time is short. Eternity matters.

So, seriously—**get up.**
Someone needs to hear the Gospel.
Someone needs your story.
Someone needs your faithfulness.

Don't stay face down in regret.

Get up! And serve the Lord with all you've got.

> **COURAGEOUS STEP:**
>
> You've likely messed up. Probably even since you started reading these devotions, and maybe even today. Ask God to forgive you. Then receive His forgiveness and get up. Extend the grace to yourself that you would extend to others, and make progress in your journey. Keep looking at Christ until you look like Christ.

Trouble in the Valley

Joshua 7:24: "And Joshua and all Israel with him took Achan the son of Zerah, and the silver and the cloak and the bar of gold, and his sons and daughters and his oxen and donkeys and sheep and his tent and all that he had. And they brought them up to the Valley of Achor."

There is trouble in the valley.

Achan saw, coveted, and took what God had commanded to be destroyed. But the consequences of his sin extended far beyond his own life. Thirty-six Israelite soldiers died in the first battle against Ai. That's potentially thirty-six wives left widowed. Thirty-six homes without a father. Thirty-six sets of parents who lost sons.

Sin is never isolated. The fallout of Achan's disobedience rippled through the entire camp.

The lesson is clear: our sin has consequences.

We might think we can get away with things, that no one will notice, or that it won't hurt anyone. But scripture tells us otherwise: *"whatever one sows, that will he also reap"* (Galatians 6:7). Sin affects relationships. It impacts those closest to us and sometimes even people we hardly know.

Think of the affair: Two families shattered. Children scarred. Trust destroyed.

Think of moral failure in leadership: A career ruined. A congregation shaken. A reputation lost.

Think of a fallen pastor: The impact reaches beyond their immediate circle to the faith of many who looked to them for guidance.

We should never put people on pedestals. But we must also acknowledge that **our sin affects others**.

In Achan's case, the impact didn't stop with the battlefield. His own family was destroyed.
That detail is hard to stomach. Why did his sons and daughters have to die?

We don't know their ages or involvement, but the text seems to imply complicity. Imagine the scene:

Achan returns to the tent with a beautiful cloak from Shinar. The family notices—they haven't seen anything like it since Egypt. *"Where did this come from, Dad?"* Perhaps his wife questions him. Then he pulls out silver and gold. *"These will provide for us once we settle in the land."* After forty years of wilderness wandering, it must have felt like finally attaining the wealth they'd been denied. Maybe they, too, began to covet. Maybe they stayed silent.

And that's the danger.

We often treat our sin casually.

We tolerate it. We rationalize it. We assume we can manage it. We forget that sin always wants more. We think giving in will satisfy, but it only increases the appetite. We focus on pleasure and ignore consequences. We minimize what God takes seriously.

But sin is never small.
Sin is always rebellion against God.
And sin always has a price.

If we saw our sin the way God sees it:

- As a breach of His commands
- As an assault on His Holiness
- As a poison infecting the people we love

Then maybe we'd be more eager to fight it.

Romans 8:13 tells us to "by the Spirit . . . put to death the deeds of the body." Or as the Puritan John Owen said: **"Be killing sin, or sin will be killing you."**

That was never more true than for Achan. His name means **"troubler,"** and his sin brought **trouble to the whole valley**. He aligned himself with what God had devoted to destruction. And in doing so, he brought judgment upon himself and his house.

So, ask yourself:

- Are you tolerating sin in your own life?
- Are you excusing what God calls evil?
- Are you inviting trouble into your valley?

God is merciful, but He is also holy. He forgives, but He also disciplines those He loves.

Take sin seriously. Confess it. Kill it. Walk in the freedom and grace that only obedience can bring, and avoid trouble in your valley.

> **COURAGEOUS STEP:**
>
> Write down your favorite sin. That's the sin that will likely prevent you from being all you can for God. Be wise and strategic. Take steps to minimize temptation. Agree with God that the sin is wrong and acknowledge that tolerating it brings trouble into your valley. Ask God to help you remove this sin from your life.

Contrasting Faith: Achan vs. Rahab

Joshua 6:25: "But Rahab the prostitute and her father's household and all who belonged to her, Joshua saved alive. And she has lived in Israel to this day, because she hid the messengers whom Joshua sent to spy out Jericho."

Are you an Achan or a Rahab?

Achan was part of the spiritual crowd. He was an Israelite, born into the covenant people of God. He had the right lineage, the right traditions, the right religious environment. From birth, he knew about the Lord. He had every advantage.

But he didn't own his faith.

He didn't trust God to provide. Instead, he took what God had forbidden. He **hid his sin**, covering it up and hoping no one would ever find out.

And when Israel was confronted with judgment? Achan stayed silent.

- When his tribe was chosen—he said nothing.
- When his clan was chosen—he said nothing.
- When his family was chosen—still nothing.

Only when he stood fully exposed did he finally confess.

Are you hiding your sin, hoping no one will discover it?

Then, there's **Rahab**.

She was a prostitute. She came from the *wrong* nation, the *wrong* background. She had *no one* encouraging her toward the God of Israel. Her way of life was far from holy.

And yet, **she believed**.

She had heard about the Lord. She knew what He had done. She recognized His power and His authority. So, when the two spies showed up, not for business but on a mission, she risked everything.

Are you trusting in God fully, knowing you can't save yourself?

She didn't betray them to her king. She hid them. She **aligned herself with God's people** and, more importantly, with God Himself.

She asked for salvation, tying a scarlet cord—a symbol of faith and a foreshadowing of Christ's blood—in her window. She couldn't save herself. She simply trusted God to do it.

Are you trusting in God fully, knowing you can't save yourself?

Do you see the contrast?

- Rahab, the outsider and harlot, became part of the people of God through faith.
- Achan, the insider and Israelite, became the object of God's judgment through disobedience.

Rahab's house, situated on the wall, should have been destroyed. But she was saved. Achan, who should have walked in victory, was buried beneath a pile of stones as a warning to others.

Which one are you?

Maybe you've grown up in the faith. Church is familiar. You know all the right answers. But you've never owned your faith. You're trusting your background, not your Savior.

Hear this: **God has no spiritual grandchildren.** You must decide for yourself whether you will trust Him.

Or maybe you've made big mistakes. Maybe you feel unworthy, like you're too flawed to be forgiven.

That's a lie. It's not about the depth of your sin. It's about the depth of God's grace. You cannot out-sin the mercy of God.

Rahab is proof. She wasn't just saved, but she became part of the family of God. She gave birth to Boaz, who redeemed Ruth. From their line came King David and, eventually, Jesus.

Only God would take Rahab the prostitute and Ruth the Moabitess and place them in the lineage of the Messiah.

What kind of faith do you have?

- The hypocritical, hidden faith of Achan?
- The flawed but genuine faith of Rahab?

The difference isn't in background, morality, or image. The difference is in **trust**.

Achan trusted himself.
Rahab trusted God.

Who are you trusting today?

COURAGEOUS STEP:

Choose authentic faith over external appearances. Stop pretending. Stop acting like you're perfect. Acknowledge your flawed faith to God and to a trusted person in your life. You don't have to be perfect. You can't be. You just need to sincerely pursue God.

Is your fear, anxiety, or despair driven by the fact that someone will find out who you really are? All humans are sinful, flawed, and in need of God's grace. Lord knows I am. You are, too. So, humbly acknowledge who you are. Now seek an authentic relationship with the God of grace.

Victory After Defeat

Joshua 8:18–19: "Then the Lord said to Joshua, 'Stretch out the javelin that is in your hand toward Ai, for I will give it into your hand.' And Joshua stretched out the javelin that was in his hand toward the city. And the men in the ambush rose quickly out of their place, and as soon as he had stretched out his hand, they ran and entered the city and captured it. And they hurried to set the city on fire."

Israel had been defeated at Ai. They had fled in fear. Joshua fell on his face before the Lord in anguish, knowing that this loss could embolden Israel's enemies. And he was right, the defeat exposed Israel's vulnerability.

But then, Joshua learned the real reason for the defeat: *God was not fighting for them.* Sin had crept into the camp. Achan had violated God's command and taken what was devoted to destruction.

There's a lesson here for us: **If God is not with us, we cannot win.** No amount of strength, strategy, or status will save us if the Lord is not on our side.

But when we humble ourselves, confess, repent, and return to the Lord, **He fights for us again.**

At Jericho, God had caused the walls to collapse. But at Ai, God used a different plan. This time, it wasn't marching and trumpets. It was military strategy. Israel would draw the enemy out and ambush them from behind.

When Joshua raised his javelin, the ambush was triggered. The city was captured. The fire was lit. **Victory after defeat.**

Don't miss this key truth: God rarely repeats Himself.

Throughout scripture, He acts in new and varied ways.

- One time, He parts the sea. Another, He piles up a river.
- One person is healed instantly. Another through doctors. Another receives ultimate healing by going home to be with the Lord.

God's methods may change, but His purposes do not. He is always faithful to His promises.

So, when we demand that God work *our* way or repeat what He did for *someone else*, we miss the point. We are the clay, not the potter. Our job isn't to dictate the method; it's to trust the Master.

Here's the hope: even after failure, God can bring victory.

So we move forward in obedience:

- We keep seeking the Lord.
- We meditate on His Word day and night.
- We walk in humility and dependence.
- We keep looking to Christ until we look like Christ.

You may have failed.
But **failure is not final** with God.
With Him, you too can experience **victory after defeat**.

COURAGEOUS STEP:

Today, realize that your relationship with God is like a long walk in the same direction. You may want a quick, easy fix that doesn't exist. The truth is that you will mess up at some level for the rest of your life on earth.

But failure is not final with God. Just like hiking a mountain. When our foot slips, we regain our footing and keep going forward. We don't roll all the way down the mountain or abandon our hike. We keep pressing for victory in Christ. We keep seeking the Lord, praying, reading our Bible, and going to church.

Uncut Stones

Joshua 8:30–31: "At that time Joshua built an altar to the Lord, the God of Israel, on Mount Ebal, just as Moses the servant of the Lord had commanded the people of Israel, as it is written in the Book of the Law of Moses, 'an altar of uncut stones, upon which no man has wielded an iron tool.' And they offered on it burnt offerings to the Lord and sacrificed peace offerings."

Why an altar of uncut stones?

Moses had written earlier in Exodus 20:25, "If you make me an altar of stone, you shall not build it of hewn stones, for if you wield your tool on it you profane it."

That's striking. Even when offering worship to God, if we touch the altar with our tools, we profane it?

Why would that be?

Because even our **best works, our finest craftsmanship, are tainted by sin.**

When Joshua built the altar at Mount Ebal, he did so *just as Moses had commanded*, using uncut stones—stones untouched by human hands. While we can't know all the reasons with certainty, we can see at least three possible purposes behind this command.

1. To guard against human pride.

God didn't want the people admiring a finely crafted altar. He didn't want them marveling at their handiwork. He wanted them to marvel at Him.

An ornate altar could shift the attention from the Creator to the creation, from God to man. But uncut stones, the raw material of the earth, left no room for boasting.

2. To separate Israel from pagan worship.

Canaanite religions often used elaborately carved altars and idols. They crafted gods in their own image and etched them into stone. By contrast, Israel's God could not be shaped, contained, or represented by human art.

An altar of uncut stones was a declaration: "We worship the unseen, holy God—not the works of our hands."

3. To highlight the holiness of God and the sinfulness of man.

The uncut stone was part of God's natural creation. Though creation was affected by the fall, it did not rebel as humanity did. It does not carry our moral guilt or sinful nature. When God commanded uncut stones for His altar, it was as if He said, *"What I have made untouched is more suitable for My presence than anything man can fashion."*

It's a sobering thought.

We're reminded of Uzzah, who reached out to steady the ark and was struck dead. Though well-intentioned, Uzzah assumed his sin-stained hands were holier than the dirt the ark might touch. They weren't.

This altar points to a deeper truth:

We have no hope of standing before a holy God on the basis of our own works. Our best efforts, best intentions, and best offerings are still corrupted by sin.

Only by God's mercy, only through the sacrifice of Jesus Christ, can we be made right.

- Our sins were laid on Him at the cross.
- His righteousness has been graciously credited to us.

So, yes, uncut stones made a better altar than our most polished attempts. Because our works cannot save us. Only God can.

What should our response be?

Humility, Gratitude, Worship.
We must see our sin for what it is.
We must see God's holiness for what it is.

And we must fall on our faces in gratitude for what Jesus has done.

Without Christ, we are hopeless. Our only hope is that our sin has been mercifully imputed on Christ at the cross, and His righteousness has been graciously imputed on us. In Christ, we are made acceptable before a holy God.

Come to the altar—not with your tools, your works, or your pride but with a heart broken by sin and amazed by grace. And worship.

COURAGEOUS STEP:

Today, admit your inability. Understand you can't do it. Your best works are marred by sin. You must rest in God's grace, knowing you can't earn His favor. God knows you completely and loves you infinitely. Humbly thank God for His grace and acceptance despite your failure.

Self-Sufficiency, Deception, and Prayerless Decisions

Joshua 9:24–25: "They answered Joshua, 'Because it was told to your servants for a certainty that the Lord your God had commanded his servant Moses to give you all the land and to destroy all the inhabitants of the land from before you—so we feared greatly for our lives because of you and did this thing. And now, behold, we are in your hand. Whatever seems good and right in your sight to do to us, do it.'"

The Lord had given Israel a miraculous victory at Jericho when the walls fell flat. After a brief setback due to Achan's sin, He delivered Ai into their hands through military strength and strategic brilliance.

As news of these victories spread, the kings west of the Jordan, those in the hill country and lowlands, recognized Israel was heading their way. They had also heard of the Lord's works in Egypt and knew Israel's mission was to devote the inhabitants of the land to destruction, just as Moses had commanded. A massive threat was coming.

So what do you do when destruction is imminent?

Rather than repent, cry out to the Lord, and plead for mercy, most of these nations chose to band together and fight a common enemy. Gibeon, however, charted a different course. Though Joshua 10 describes Gibeon as a great city—like one of the royal cities, greater than Ai, and filled with warriors—they concluded that resistance was futile.

So, they got creative. But instead of appealing to the mercy of Israel and Yahweh with honesty, they turned to deception. Knowing that Israel was permitted to make treaties with distant nations, they disguised themselves as such.

Perhaps today, they would have scoured thrift shops and perhaps even dumpsters. In their day, they gathered old sacks for their donkeys, patched wineskins, worn-out sandals, tattered clothes, and dry, crumbly bread.

They carefully crafted their story, pretending to come from a distant land, too far away to have heard of the recent victories at Jericho and Ai. They even included theological flattery: *"We have heard of the name of the Lord your God."* And four times in the ninth chapter, they refer to themselves as *"your servants"* (vv. 8, 9, 11, 24).

But where was Joshua's discernment? Did he not wonder why these people hadn't appeared during the 40 years of Israel's wandering? Why didn't he stop to seek the Lord in prayer?

Instead, Joshua and the leaders relied on their own understanding. The visitors' story sounded plausible. Their flattery was appealing. Their appearance seemed authentic.

The Israelites investigated, but only with their eyes and ears, not through seeking wisdom from God. **They were self-sufficient.** They thought, "*We've got this.*"

Some of the greatest mistakes in my life have stemmed from self-sufficiency. When I assume I have everything under control, God often reminds me that I don't. When I fail to stop and pray, He allows challenges that drive me back to Him.

How much better would our lives be if we simply sought God first? But pride tells us to act like we have it all together. We want others to think we know what we're doing. We resist humbling ourselves to ask God for wisdom or admit we need help. And yet, in His grace, God gives us this story—from one of the greatest leaders in scripture—as a reminder: **no one can do it alone.**

After the victory at Ai, a win that required strategy and skill, I imagine some Israelites were praising Joshua. Maybe someone even made a meme on Instagram comparing him to Moses. The headlines might have read: *"Greatest Military Victory Yet—Led by Israel's Genius Commander."*

Perhaps you've also started believing the press around you. Maybe after a recent success, you're thinking, "*I've got this . . . I don't need God.*" Be careful. It's in such moments that we are **most vulnerable to defeat.** Proverbs 16:18 tells us that pride and self-sufficiency often precede a fall.

So, seek the Lord in prayer. Stay humble. Ask Him for wisdom from above. Whether you find yourself tempted to deceive like the Gibeonites or to rely on your own strength like the Israelites, learn the lesson of Joshua 9: **trust in God, not in your own understanding.**

> **COURAGEOUS STEP:**
> Today, acknowledge that you trust yourself too much. You trust in your ability, your intelligence, your work. You might not pray because you think you can handle it. Then, fear, anxiety, and despair return because you stopped trusting God and started doing it yourself. Seek God's wisdom today, and don't rely on your own understanding.

Keeping Your Word

Joshua 9:18: "But the people of Israel did not attack them, because the leaders of the congregation had sworn to them by the Lord, the God of Israel. Then all the congregation murmured against the leaders."

Joshua had been deceived. The Gibeonites tricked him, and only three days later did he learn that they were neighbors, not foreigners. The Israelites immediately set out and reached the Gibeonite cities. Joshua realized his mistake. Perhaps due to self-sufficiency and a prayerless decision, he had made peace with a people he was meant to destroy.

What would you have done in his place? Would you have broken the treaty on the grounds that it was based on lies? Would you have destroyed the Gibeonites as just punishment for their deception? That's exactly what modern society might deem fair. But Christians are called to a higher standard—**we are called to keep our word.**

The congregation murmured, and understandably so. From their perspective, the leaders had failed. No one could yet see that God would use this situation for Israel's good. No one knew that He would soon hand over five enemy kings, outside their fortified cities, and accelerate the conquest of the land. All they knew was that peace had been made with the wrong people.

To his credit, Joshua didn't cave to popular opinion. He didn't reverse course to appease the crowd. Instead, **he honored his commitment**, even to his own hurt. This passage teaches us something vital: while we should always seek God in prayer before making decisions, there will be times when we act with incomplete information. In those moments, **we must be people of integrity.** Christians walk in truth, and even when it costs us, we keep our word.

The world keeps its promises when it's convenient. But Christians demonstrate their devotion to the God who never lies by keeping our word, even when it's hard.

And you know what? God blessed Israel for it. In His grace, He allowed the Gibeonites to become part of Israel. Nehemiah tells us that after the exile, Gibeonites were among those who returned to help rebuild the temple.

God used Israel to bless outsiders like Rahab, Caleb, and now the Gibeonites. He also used the treaty to draw out Israel's enemies.

Notice: The kings of Canaan didn't initially gather to fight Israel. They united to punish Gibeon for making peace with Israel. Joshua could have stood by and let them be destroyed as just reward for their deception.

Instead, he honored the treaty and marched all night to defend them. The kings who sought to crush Gibeon found themselves fighting not just Israel but the living God. They were defeated by hailstones and a miraculously extended day orchestrated by the God of Israel.

Isn't that just like God? He takes our **mistakes** and turns them into **blessings.**

So, trust Him. Keep your word. And then wait and see how God works.

Whether it benefits us or costs us, **Christians must be known as people who keep their word.**

He takes our mistakes and turns them into blessings.

COURAGEOUS STEP:

Today, honor your commitments. If you need to make something right or apologize for not keeping your word to a friend, do so. Going forward, remember that Christians keep their word, so be wise about what you commit to do, and talk to God about every decision in your life, asking Him to provide you with wisdom.

Tragedy Into Triumph

Joshua 10:42: "And Joshua captured all these kings and their land at one time, because the Lord God of Israel fought for Israel."

Joshua had made a major mistake. He failed to seek God in prayer, and as a result, he was deceived by the Gibeonites. Thinking they were from a distant land, he made a treaty with them, only to learn three days later that they lived nearby in a region God had commanded to be destroyed.

What happened next is remarkable. Five kings formed an alliance to attack Gibeon, perhaps to punish them for the treaty, or perhaps because of Gibeon's strategic location. In desperation, Gibeon sent an urgent plea to Joshua: *"Come up to us quickly and save us!"* (Joshua 10:6). It was their only hope.

Now imagine yourself in Joshua's place. What would you do? Would you refuse to help and let the deceivers face the consequences? Would you delay your response, citing the need to review recent treaties? Would you quietly take revenge by doing nothing?

Joshua didn't hold a grudge. He didn't respond with bitterness or pettiness. Instead, he gathered his mighty men of valor. And then God spoke: *"Do not fear them, for I have given them into your hands"* (Joshua 10:8). **Notice the past tense—God had already secured the victory.**

Joshua marched all night. It was a grueling 20-mile journey with an elevation gain of 4,000 feet. For seasoned hikers, that's an eight- to ten-hour trek. After that exhausting night, Joshua led his army directly into battle. Scripture says they "came upon them suddenly." The Lord threw the enemy into confusion, and Israel struck them with a decisive blow at Gibeon.

Now look at what God did.

He used Joshua's mistake to draw out five powerful armies from their fortified cities, allowing Israel to defeat them all at once. Because Joshua responded rightly to his error, he participated in one of the most incredible victories in all of scripture. He failed forward. He didn't let one mistake lead to another. He didn't spiral into defeat.

God took a failure and made it a masterpiece. He turned tragedy into triumph.

And He does the same for us. He takes our pain and gives it purpose. He takes our mistakes and turns them into platforms for His glory—*if* we allow Him.

The real question is: How will we respond? Will we take revenge when wronged? Will we get bitter or passive? Will we let hurt and regret paralyze us from doing what's right?

Joshua didn't. He stayed the course. He pursued God's plan. It took sacrifice. He marched all night and fought a hard battle. But it was a battle that **God had already won.**

We too fight battles that God has already won through Christ. Are we willing to pursue Him, to do the hard work, to trust Him in the aftermath of our mistakes?

Joshua failed forward, and saw God do something amazing.

The next time you fall short, remember: **God isn't finished.** Fail forward. Trust Him. Stay the course. And watch Him turn your tragedy into triumph.

> ### COURAGEOUS STEP:
> Fail Forward. Don't be paralyzed by mistakes. Trust that God can redeem them and perhaps even use them to help others. Don't repeat them, creating a cycle of failure, but keep moving forward on your journey of strong and courageous faith.

When God Acts

Joshua 10:11: "And as they fled before Israel, while they were going down the ascent of Beth-horon, the Lord threw down large stones from heaven on them as far as Azekah, and they died. There were more who died because of the hailstones than the sons of Israel killed with the sword."

Twice in Joshua 10, we're told that "the Lord fought for Israel" (vv. 14, 42). Because of this divine intervention, Israel overcame overwhelming odds and defeated a numerically superior enemy.

In this remarkable battle, God hurled hailstones from heaven, killing more enemy soldiers than Israel did with the sword. Even more astonishing, at Joshua's request, God lengthened the day so that it appeared the sun stood still in the sky. The text states that there has never been a day like it "when the Lord heeded the voice of a man" (Joshua 10:14).

What can we learn from this in our own time? We may not expect God to send hailstones on our enemies or literally lengthen our days. He certainly has the power, but scripture shows us that He rarely repeats miracles in exactly the same way. The Canaanite nations had rejected God for centuries, and this was a moment of divine judgment.

Yet, this passage gives us at least three powerful truths to hold on to:

1. **God hears the prayers of His servants.**
2. **God has the power to do whatever He pleases.**
3. **God alone deserves the credit for success.**

First, the author of Joshua surprises us. He could have focused on the most dramatic elements of the story: the hailstones or the sun standing still. But instead, he emphasizes this: *"the Lord heeded the voice of a man."* In order to respond, God must first hear.

Let that sink in. The God who created and sustains the universe—the God who knows all, sees all, and controls all—**hears your prayers.** He listens when you cry out to Him. You can ask Him to help, to guide, to provide, and to comfort. And He hears you because He loves you.

Too often, we take this privilege for granted. Instead of going to God first, we go to social media, we gossip, or we stew in worry. But prayer should be our first response, not our last resort.

Second, **God has the power to answer.** I don't know what you're facing, but I know God is able to overcome it. He may not always answer in the way we hope. He may say *no*. He may say *slow* because the timing isn't right. Or He may say *go*. Regardless of the answer, don't doubt His power.

Sometimes, the very act of coming to Him repeatedly is part of the process of drawing closer to Him. And remember, even if God doesn't heal or deliver in this life, He will in the next. Nothing happens to a child of God that a good resurrection won't fix.

Third, **God deserves the praise.** Anything we accomplish in life, any success, growth, or victory, comes from Him. He gives the gifts, the strength, the opportunities, and even the breath we use to achieve it.

Notice that the author doesn't commend Joshua's spirituality or Israel's ambition. He doesn't say Israel won because they were strong or wise. He says **Israel won because God fought for them.**

How often do we fall into the trap of pride, pounding our proverbial chest, thinking we've achieved something on our own? Scripture warns us that pride comes before the fall, but God exalts the humble in due time.

If you want to flourish in your life, here's the path:

- **Talk to God**—He hears.
- **Trust His power**—He can act.
- **Stay humble**—Give Him the praise.

That is the life of a faithful servant. That is a life well-lived.

COURAGEOUS STEP:

Today's courageous step is to give God the glory for everything. All of your gifts, including the breath in your lungs, God provided. Without God, you can do nothing. So you cannot be a glory thief. In genuine humility, you must give God the credit and glory for all victories.

Joshua Obeyed

Joshua 11:15: "Just as the Lord had commanded Moses his servant, so Moses commanded Joshua, and so Joshua did. He left nothing undone of all that the Lord had commanded Moses."

"He left nothing undone." What a remarkable statement.

The author emphasizes this point repeatedly:

- "Joshua did to them just as the Lord said" (11:9).
- "Just as Moses the servant of the Lord had commanded" (11:12).
- "Just as the Lord had commanded" (11:15).
- "Just as the Lord commanded Moses" (11:20).
- "According to all that the Lord had spoken to Moses" (11:23).

In one chapter, five separate statements affirm Joshua's complete obedience. It would be easy to glance at these phrases and quickly conclude, "We should obey, too," and move on. But to do so would miss the richness and weight of what's being said.

Joshua obeyed consistently throughout his life and leadership. He erected memorial stones after crossing the Jordan to remind Israel of God's faithfulness. He ensured that defeated kings were removed before sundown, just as Deuteronomy commanded. He honored a flawed treaty with the Gibeonites even after their deception, marching all night to defend them. He dealt decisively with sin in the camp when Achan disobeyed God. He concluded his leadership with a bold challenge, *"choose this day whom you will serve,"* (Joshua 24:15) and a warning that even the rocks would bear witness if Israel broke covenant with the Lord.

Joshua's story is a testimony of **detailed obedience**.

But let's go even deeper. Did Joshua obey perfectly? Not exactly. He allowed sin to linger in the camp when Achan's disobedience went unnoticed, which resulted in a military defeat and the loss of lives. He failed to pray before making a treaty with the Gibeonites and was deceived. So why does the author say Joshua left nothing undone?

Because Joshua **failed forward**. He didn't dwell on failure; he learned from it. He grew in faith, humbled himself, and pursued God's commands with increasing passion and precision. He didn't make the same mistakes again. His life wasn't marked by perfection but by **faithful, growing obedience**.

Consider the timeline of the conquest. Based on Caleb's age, the northern military campaign likely took seven years. That means for seven long, hard years, an aging Joshua led Israel in battle to fulfill God's commands. He didn't quit. He didn't claim he'd done enough. He didn't retire early. He pressed on to finish the work God gave him.

Joshua left nothing undone.

Now ask yourself: *What am I leaving undone?*

- What sin have I failed to put to death?
- What step of obedience am I avoiding?
- What calling have I delayed because I lacked faith?

Remember the repeated encouragement from God to Joshua and from Joshua to the people:

"Do not be afraid or dismayed; be strong and courageous" (Joshua 10:25).

Our God is with us. He is strong enough to accomplish whatever He calls us to do.

So make a list, identify the areas where obedience is incomplete, and start working through them.

Let's be the kind of Christ-followers who **leave nothing undone** of all that the Lord has commanded us.

COURAGEOUS STEP:

What have you left undone? What has God asked you to do that remains unfinished or unstarted? Take one step toward completing it today.

The Lord Controls All

Joshua 11:20: "For it was the Lord's doing to harden their hearts that they should come against Israel in battle, in order that they should be devoted to destruction and should receive no mercy but be destroyed, just as the Lord commanded Moses."

"It's not my fault."

If you're like me, you've said that before and probably more than once. We are quick to shift the blame. Eve blamed the serpent. Adam blamed Eve, and, to some degree, even blamed God for giving Eve to him. We blame our circumstances, our upbringing, our genetics, our stress, or even God Himself.

This verse might tempt us to do just that. If God is in control of all things, can we really be held responsible? Should we say "God made me do it" rather than "the Devil made me do it"?

But as students of scripture, we must interpret unclear passages in light of the clear ones. This isn't the first time we've encountered language about God hardening hearts. In

Exodus, we're told that God hardened Pharaoh's heart *and* that Pharaoh hardened his own heart. Scripture shows both divine sovereignty and human responsibility.

The nations Israel defeated had centuries to repent. In fact, Abraham's descendants had to wait 400 years to inherit the land because, as Genesis 15:16 says, *"the iniquity of the Amorites is not yet complete."* Even after Israel left Egypt, these nations had time—and reason—to fear the Lord. Rahab heard and believed, and she received grace. The Gibeonites, even through deception, sought peace and were spared.

But the rest rebelled. Knowing that Yahweh fought for Israel, they didn't repent. They resisted. They gathered to fight against God's people. Unlike Nineveh, they did not listen to the warning.

And **God gave them what they had chosen.** He allowed them to persist in rebellion, and then He solidified their decision. He completed what they started. The result was judgment.

Verses like this can seem harsh until we remember the full character of God. The New Testament tells us God is "not willing that any should perish, but that all should come to repentance" (2 Peter 3:9). He is "slow to anger, and abounding in steadfast love" (Exodus 34:6). And yet, He is also just. The time had come to judge those who had sacrificed their children, image-bearers of God, to false gods. His patience had not been short; it had been more than generous.

This should terrify us. **It is a sobering thing to fall into the hands of a holy God without grace.**

Most people reading this devotional probably aren't shaking their fists at God in outright rebellion. The very fact that you're reading suggests a desire to follow Him. But passages like this should awaken us to the urgency of the Gospel for those who remain in darkness.

There are still nations, cities, and individuals with little or no access to the truth. Today, people continue to sacrifice their children, not always on literal altars, but to idols of convenience, comfort, materialism, or personal autonomy. **God will not be mocked. What we sow, we will reap.**

This should break our hearts. It should stir up sorrow over human rebellion and urgency for the lost. It should ignite a passion for evangelism and missions. We are stewards of the truth, and the world is running full speed toward destruction.

As long as someone is still breathing, the possibility for repentance remains. Don't give up. Keep praying. Keep sharing. All of us are destined for either eternal mercy or eternal judgment.

And in our own lives, let's not minimize our sin or make excuses for it. Let's be quick to repent, eager to receive forgiveness, and committed to living in a way that points others to the Lord who controls all.

COURAGEOUS STEP:

Evaluate your heart. Do you blame others for everything or even some things that go wrong in your life? Do you ever own the blame? Mature leaders shoulder the blame and share the praise. Mature Christians don't blame others for everything. Part of our journey is owning our mistakes and learning from them. Today, admit your mistakes, and commit to stop blaming everyone else.

Failure to Conquer

Joshua 13:13: "Yet the people of Israel did not drive out the Geshurites or the Maacathites, but Geshur and Maacath dwell in the midst of Israel to this day."

Joshua 16:10: "However, they did not drive out the Canaanites who lived in Gezer, so the Canaanites have lived in the midst of Ephraim to this day but have been made to do forced labor."

Joshua 17:12–13: "Yet the people of Manasseh could not take possession of those cities, but the Canaanites persisted in dwelling in that land. Now when the people of Israel grew strong, they put the Canaanites to forced labor, but did not utterly drive them out."

Over and over again, we're told that the **Israelites did not drive out the enemy.** At first glance, it seems understandable, especially in the case of the tribe of Joseph, who encountered Canaanites equipped with iron chariots.

But the problem becomes clear when we read Joshua 13:6, where God promises, "I myself will drive them out from before the people of Israel." Was God not powerful enough? That can't be the explanation. We've already seen Him stop the Jordan River, bring down the walls of Jericho, lengthen a day, and destroy armies with hailstones. God's power was never in question.

The issue wasn't divine weakness; it was human unbelief.

Joshua confronts the tribe of Joseph in Joshua 17:17b–18, reminding them, "You are a numerous people and have great power . . . you shall drive out the Canaanites, though they have chariots of iron, and though they are strong."

Yet their complaint sounds eerily familiar: *"The enemy is too strong."* It echoes the report of the ten fearful spies from decades earlier. Their failure came, first, from **a lack of faith in God's power**.

But there's another problem: Joshua 17:13 tells us that when Israel grew strong, they "put the Canaanites to forced labor, but did not utterly drive them out." So, they had the strength but not the will. They preferred comfort and convenience to full obedience. Servants were more appealing than surrender. They made peace with their enemy rather than eliminating the threat.

We don't fight Canaanites today, but we do face a very real enemy: the devil, sin, and the patterns of this fallen world. And too often, we make the same mistake. We don't put our sin to death. We tolerate it. Excuse it. Justify it. We make peace with it.

Is the Holy Spirit not strong enough to help us? Or is it that we love our sin more than we love our Savior? Do we overestimate the strength of our sin and underestimate the strength of our Deliverer?

What's the big deal if we hang on to a few "harmless" sins?

Read the book of Judges.

In Judges 2:2–3, God rebukes Israel: "You have not obeyed my voice . . . I will not drive them out before you, but they shall become thorns in your sides, and their gods shall be a snare to you." Then, in verse 14, we're told that "the anger of the Lord was kindled against Israel," and, in verse 15, that "the hand of the Lord was against them for harm."

The point is clear: making peace with sin gives the enemy a foothold in our lives. It becomes a thorn in our side and a snare for our hearts. It grieves the Holy Spirit, angers our Savior, and robs us of victory.

Israel eventually faced exile and slavery. Are we willing to live as slaves to our sin?

It's time to make war.

By the power of the Spirit, we are called to *put to death the deeds of the flesh* (Romans 8:13). We must not repeat Israel's failure. Instead, let us follow the greater Joshua: Jesus, who conquered sin and death and offers us victory through His resurrection.

Don't make peace with your sin. Make war. Fight it. Kill it. And walk in the freedom Christ has secured for you.

> **COURAGEOUS STEP:**
>
> Stop making peace with sin. Identify one area where you've grown complacent and commit to a spiritual battle by the power of the Spirit that lives within us. If you have a trusted Christian friend, ask that person to help you make progress in this area.

Balaam Dies

Joshua 13:22: "Balaam also, the son of Beor, the one who practiced divination, was killed with the sword by the people of Israel among the rest of their slain."

If you've read Numbers 22, you know about Balaam and his talking donkey, but have you ever noticed that Balaam is specifically mentioned among the slain in Joshua 13:22? This verse reflects a summary of earlier events from Numbers 31.

Why is Balaam singled out here? Joshua didn't personally kill him, and the news wasn't new.

Balaam is a complex, even confusing, figure in scripture. In Numbers 22, he's summoned and hired by Balak to curse Israel. God initially tells him not to go but then permits him in verse 20, only to become angry that Balaam went (v. 22).

Why the shift? Likely because Balaam's heart was bent toward personal profit rather than obedience. He was going through the motions, but his motives were corrupt.

When Balaam finally delivers his oracles, he surprisingly blesses Israel instead of cursing them. In Numbers 24:1–2, it even says that Balaam "saw that it pleased the Lord" and that "the Spirit of God came upon him." Does this mean Balaam was a true believer? Not at all. God can and does use unbelievers to accomplish His purposes when He desires. The Spirit came upon Balaam not to affirm him but to speak through him.

Later scriptures help us understand Balaam's true character:

- *Micah 6:5* remembers God's faithfulness in not allowing Balaam to curse Israel.
- *2 Peter 2:15* condemns Balaam as one "who loved gain from wrongdoing."
- *Jude 1:11* includes Balaam's error in a list of corrupt examples.
- *Revelation 2:14* rebukes the church in Pergamum for following "the teaching of Balaam," who advised Balak to put a stumbling block before Israel by leading them into idolatry and sexual immorality.

While Balaam never explicitly cursed Israel, he did something worse: he counseled Balak on how to seduce Israel into sin with Moabite women at Peor. As a result, twenty-four thousand Israelites died in a divine plague (Numbers 25:9).

Balaam is the tragic story of someone **spiritually gifted but morally compromised**. He had genuine spiritual insight. He spoke with God (Numbers 22:9) and gave oracles with impressive theological content. But for all his knowledge and giftedness, Balaam was driven by greed and self-interest. He manipulated spiritual realities for personal gain, even at the cost of others' lives.

That's why the author of Joshua brings up Balaam again. He's a warning.

Just because someone is gifted doesn't mean they are godly. Just because someone can speak spiritual truths doesn't mean they know or love the Lord.

So what about you?

Are you gifted? Do you possess spiritual insight, teaching ability, leadership, or influence? Are you tempted to use those gifts for your own advantage rather than for God's purposes?

Balaam teaches us this: **gifts without godliness lead to ruin**.
We must develop *character* that matches our *calling*.
We must pursue *intimacy with God* before *activity for God*.
We must resist the temptation to use our gifts in a way that promotes self rather than glorifies Christ.

In the end, Balaam died, like everyone else. Despite his gifts, his insight, and his fame, he fell under judgment.

So will we, unless we walk in humility and faithfulness.

Use your gifts, but don't worship them. Be a faithful steward. Walk closely with God. And remember, even someone as gifted as Balaam still dies.

COURAGEOUS STEP:

Focus on developing godly character and not just gifts. Identify areas of weakness in your personal character. Do you lie, exaggerate, get angry, try to please people more than God, or desire power or prestige? Spend time this week in the Word pursuing deeper intimacy with God before you pursue public activity for God.

Wholly Followed God

Joshua 14:8–9, 14: "But my brothers who went up with me made the heart of the people melt; yet I wholly followed the Lord my God. And Moses swore on that day, saying, 'Surely the land on which your foot has trodden shall be an inheritance for you and your children forever, because you have wholly followed the Lord my God.' . . . Therefore Hebron became the inheritance of Caleb the son of Jephunneh the Kenizzite to this day, because he wholly followed the Lord, the God of Israel."

Caleb wholly followed the Lord.

Scripture highlights this rare and admirable quality multiple times (Numbers 14:24, Numbers 32:12, and Deuteronomy 1:36), each affirming that Caleb had a "different spirit" and followed God *fully*.

What made Caleb different? He wholly followed the Lord.

But what does that actually look like?

1. Conviction to Take a Stand

Caleb was one of only two spies who brought back a faithful report and trusted that God would give Israel the land. While the others magnified the problem, Caleb magnified the promise. He followed the Lord. When he quieted the crowd and spoke in favor of advancing, they wanted to stone him. He demonstrated a bold willingness to risk his life for the sake of obedience.

2. Consistency in Walking by Faith

In Joshua 14, Caleb repeatedly acknowledges the Lord. Verses 6, 8, 9, 10, and 12 all remind us of Caleb's faith in Him. He believed the Lord had kept him alive for a purpose. That's no small belief when almost everyone from your generation has passed away. He gave God credit for his strength and looked to the Lord for victory.

Caleb walked by faith, not by sight. And he wasn't looking for easy battles.

3. Confidence to Be Bold for God

"Now give me this hill country" (Joshua 14:12).

Caleb's request at 85 years old was not for rest, not for comfort, not for ease, but for the most difficult territory. The Anakim, the giants, lived there. Their cities were heavily fortified. Hebron, the greatest stronghold, was before him.

Yet Caleb didn't shrink back. He faced giants and conquered them. The text even names the three sons of Anak, Sheshai,

Ahiman, and Talmai, whom Caleb drove out. It took forty-five years, but he did what he knew God had empowered him to do.

4. An Example to Follow

Caleb's faith had a generational impact. His daughter boldly made a request of her own, no doubt influenced by her father's courage (Joshua 15:16-19). His nephew, Othniel, later conquered a difficult land and became his son-in-law. Later, Othniel became Israel's first judge and gave the land rest for forty years (Judges 3:9-11). 2 Timothy 2:2 reminds us to entrust truth to faithful people who will teach others. Caleb passed on his bold faith to the next generation.

You may be tempted to think, *"I could never be a Caleb."* But did you know Caleb probably wasn't even an Israelite by blood? He is repeatedly called "the son of Jephunneh the Kenizzite." Yet God used him just as He used Rahab.

God can use anyone who wholly follows Him.

Caleb waited 45 years. He wandered with the faithless, endured hardship, fought with Joshua, and never lost sight of God's promise. And when the time came, he was ready. He didn't hesitate. He believed. He conquered. He wholly followed the Lord.

Are you willing to wholly follow the Lord, even if it takes forty-five years to see the promise fulfilled?

God is still looking for people like Caleb.

COURAGEOUS STEP:

Choose one area today where you can follow God more fully in your thoughts, words, or actions. For example, are you using your words to tear people down or make fun of them rather than build them up? Are your thoughts glorifying God and benefiting others? Do your actions reflect God's commands? Maybe you need to join a local church, start serving there, be baptized, or start giving back to God part of what He has given to you.

Unfinished Task

Joshua 13:13: "Yet the people of Israel did not drive out."

Have you ever grown satisfied with past victories and complacent about future challenges in your life?

The book of Joshua repeatedly highlights an unfinished task. In Joshua 13, the eastern tribes failed to drive out the Geshurites and the Maacathites. The result? These enemies continued to dwell among them.

In Joshua 15:63, we read that the people of Judah "could not drive out" the Jebusites. But why not? God had already promised to drive them out. Did they rely on their own strength instead of trusting God's power? Are we guilty of doing the same, trying to conquer sin in our own effort rather than depending on the Spirit?

In Joshua 16:10 and again in 17:12–13, we learn that Israel "did not drive out" the Canaanites but instead made them do forced labor. That decision speaks volumes. If they had the strength to enslave their enemies, they likely had the strength to expel them. Why didn't they? Perhaps they preferred the comfort of having others do the hard work. Perhaps they rationalized that some enemies weren't worth the effort to remove.

How often do we do the same with our sin?
We tolerate it.
We manage it.
We make peace with it.
Rather than viewing sin as an enemy to destroy, we treat it as a discomfort to control, a private indulgence to manage rather than a threat to eliminate.

In Joshua 17:17–18, the tribe of Joseph complained that they couldn't drive out the Canaanites because they had iron chariots and were strong. But God had already declared victory. The issue wasn't God's ability; it was their lack of faith. They looked at the size of the problem instead of the power of their God.

Do we do the same?

We look at the addictive nature of our sin, the mountain of change required, and we give up before we start. We resign ourselves to a defeated life—never asking, never trusting, never fighting. But we aren't called to passive faith. We are called to **strong and courageous** faith.

"Be killing sin, or sin will be killing you."–John Owen

In Joshua 18:3, Joshua asks a pointed question: **"How long will you put off going in to take possession of the land?"**

So let me ask you: how long will you put off making war against your sin?

"Be killing sin, or sin will be killing you."—John Owen

What sins have you been tolerating? Lying, gossip, exaggeration, lust, pornography, gluttony, greed, laziness, fear, anxiety, bitterness, coveting, anger, pride?

Maybe you think, *"I've got it under control; it's not doing serious harm."* But that's not what scripture teaches.

The consequences of compromise are clear in the book of Judges. When we make peace with sin, we invite spiritual thorns and snares into our lives. We weaken ourselves and grieve the Spirit of God. The cycle of the book of Judges repeats itself. The people sin. God gives them over to their enemies. They repent and cry out to God. God rescues them with a Judge. A new generation arises that does not know. They repeat the same cycle.

Let's break the cycle.

It's time to finish the unfinished task. It's time to "decide" to **make war**.

The phrase *de* means *off*. The word *-cide* means *to kill*. Insecticide. Pesticide. Germicide. Each one exists to destroy. That's what we must do with our sin—decide to put it to death by the power of the Spirit.

Develop a plan. Take it seriously. Go to war.

Don't leave sin unconquered. Don't live with an unfinished task. Finish what God has empowered you to finish.

> **COURAGEOUS STEP:**
>
> You may be thinking, we have already covered overcoming sin. Correct. But scripture shows us that resisting temptation and conquering sin in our lives is a struggle that will not end in this life. I suspect you either failed or ignored the warning. Today, make a plan to have victory over the temptation you fall to most frequently.

Daughters

Joshua 17:3–4: "Now Zelophehad the son of Hepher, son of Gilead, son of Machir, son of Manasseh, had no sons, but only daughters, and these are the names of his daughters: Mahlah, Noah, Hoglah, Milcah, and Tirzah."

Daughters!

As the father of a daughter, I know firsthand the unique place daughters hold in a father's heart. In the book of Joshua, we encounter a powerful story involving five daughters of a man named Zelophehad. He had no sons, only daughters, and his name might have disappeared from Israel's inheritance records if not for their boldness and God's gracious provision.

These five daughters approached Eleazar the priest and Joshua, reminding them of what the Lord had commanded Moses: that they should receive an inheritance. Joshua honored the request and gave them land among the tribe of Manasseh.

Their story, first introduced in Numbers 27, tells us that their father died in the wilderness, not in rebellion with Korah, but *"for his own sin"* (Numbers 27:3). We don't know the details, but whatever the cause, it didn't disqualify him from being remembered or his daughters from receiving God's blessing.

Look at the **grace of God** in this situation:

- God granted Zelophehad a **lasting inheritance** through his daughters despite his sin.
- God provided **provision and protection** for the daughters by securing their inheritance.
- God used their case to issue a **command for all of Israel**: if a man dies with no sons, his inheritance is to go to his daughters.

This is a beautiful reminder of God's **value and care for women**, especially in a cultural context where women were often undervalued. This ruling, recorded in scripture, shows that God affirms the worth of both sons and daughters, offering dignity and legacy to both.

Some today argue that any difference in role implies inequality. But God created male and female as equal in worth and value, both made in His image yet with distinct responsibilities. Here in Joshua, we see that **distinction does not equal devaluation**. These daughters are honored, protected, and used by God to shape future generations of inheritance law in Israel.

To ensure that their land stayed within the tribal allotments, the daughters were instructed to marry sons of their father's brothers, and they obeyed, which preserved the inheritance within the tribe of Manasseh.

In a time and culture where women were often overlooked, God highlighted these women and upheld their place among His people. He included them in scripture.

Jesus followed the same pattern. He treated women with dignity and compassion. Women supported His ministry, stood near the cross, and were the first witnesses to the resurrection. In God's Kingdom, there is no second class.

If you view women as objects or infer their value from cultural stereotypes, you have a spiritual problem. **All people, male and female, are made in the image of God.** Jesus died to save all people, and in Christ, we are brothers and sisters. While scripture clearly calls men to lead their families and serve as elders in the church, women have an equally valuable role in the ministry of the Gospel.

Titus 2 and Proverbs 31 outline beautiful, powerful pictures of faithful women shaping homes, serving in churches, and impacting the generations. We should encourage more women to pursue theological education and become strong, faithful disciplers in the roles God has called them to.

And don't miss the daughters' approach: They **appealed to the authority of God's Word.** They didn't come with entitlement but with conviction grounded in scripture. They believed God's Word delivered through Moses mattered, and they expected it to be honored.

That's a lesson for all of us. Whether we like it or not, God's Word has authority. We don't sit in judgment of scripture, picking and choosing what we like. Scripture sits in judgment over us.

These daughters, God's daughters, Mahlah, Noah, Hoglah, Milcah, and Tirzah, stand as examples of strong and courageous faith.

> **COURAGEOUS STEP:**
>
> Honor someone today who is not like you. Choose someone who doesn't often receive praise. Make a decision that in your actions, you will value all life because we are all created in God's image. If you can't think of someone, have a conversation with someone you don't know to learn more about them.

Ungrateful & Entitled

Joshua 17:14: "Then the people of Joseph spoke to Joshua, saying, 'Why have you given me but one lot and one portion as an inheritance, although I am a numerous people, since all along the Lord has blessed me?'"

Have you ever complained about a gift?

Most of us have, whether we said it out loud or not. We receive a raise at work but immediately think it's not enough. Someone gives us a present, but it's not quite what we wanted. We earn an award, but it's not the one we were hoping for. Or maybe we see someone else succeed with a job offer, an engagement, or a new house, but instead of celebrating with them, we sulk.

This is what happens with the tribe of Joseph in Joshua 17. They complain: "Why have you given me but one lot and one portion?" (Joshua 17:14). Then they justify their dissatisfaction: We are "a numerous people." That prideful statement will come back to bite them.

Joshua responds with clarity: "If you are a numerous people, go up by yourselves to the forest, and there clear ground for yourselves" (Joshua 17:15). But the people push back again.

"The hill country is not enough"... and the Canaanites have "chariots of iron" (Joshua 17:15-16). My translation: "We want more, and we don't want to do the hard work or face the challenge."

Joshua doesn't let them off the hook. He doubles down, telling them that if they are numerous and strong, then go clear the forest. Later, he challenges them to drive out the Canaanites even though they have chariots of iron and are strong (Joshua 17:15, 18).

I imagine Joshua thinking, "Really? Chariots of iron? After everything God has done? He stopped the waters of the Jordan. Brought down Jericho's walls. Used hailstones to defeat armies. Stopped the sun in the sky. Have you forgotten Merom? Chariots are no obstacle for the living God!"

The tribe of Joseph, sadly, contrasts with the faith of Joshua. Joshua modeled strong and courageous faith. Though he made mistakes, he failed forward. He did the hard things, honored God, and gave Him the glory for every victory. The tribe of Joseph didn't.

They were **ungrateful**—unwilling to embrace what they'd been given because it required work.

They were **entitled**—demanding more while ignoring God's power to help them conquer what was already theirs.

How often do we do the same?

Instead of thanking God for what we've been given, we scroll social media and compare ourselves to others. We throw silent pity parties, looking at curated highlight reels and wondering why our lives don't measure up. Rather than working for God with joy and gratitude, we grow discontent, focused on what we don't have rather than the abundance we do.

This mindset is fueled by a culture that constantly tells us we need more to be happy. But we're called to contentment in Christ.

Let's take time today to refocus.

- Thank God for the gifts He's already given, big and small.
- Reflect on His past faithfulness and provision.
- Remember the ultimate gift: Jesus paid the price for our sin, conquered the grave, and gave us purpose through salvation.

We were created for good works. We each have a unique race to run, and the Lord is with us in it. So let's fix our eyes on Jesus, the author and perfecter of our faith, and **live with gratitude**, not entitlement.

COURAGEOUS STEP:

Send a text, email, or even better, a handwritten note, to thank someone for something they did. Show gratitude to someone for a task you frequently take for granted. Step forward in being a person who rejects entitlement and shows gratitude. Your life and the lives of those around you will be better for it.

Justice and Mercy

Joshua 20:3–4; 9: "That the manslayer who strikes any person without intent or unknowingly may flee there. They shall be for you a refuge from the avenger of blood. He shall flee to one of these cities and shall stand at the entrance of the gate of the city and explain his case to the elders of that city. Then they shall take him into the city and give him a place, and he shall remain with them . . . These were the cities designated for all the people of Israel and for the stranger sojourning among them, that anyone who killed a person without intent could flee there, so that he might not die by the hand of the avenger of blood, till he stood before the congregation."

How do you know what someone truly values?

Spend enough time around them, and you'll see it—not just in what they say, but in how they live, the choices they make, and the systems they put in place.

In Joshua 20, God establishes a system called the **cities of refuge**. This system and the values it reflects show us clearly that God loves **justice and mercy**.

These cities weren't a minor footnote. They're described in Exodus, Numbers, Deuteronomy, and Joshua. They're repeated four times in scripture because the message matters: **God is both just and merciful.**

The Design of Refuge

According to Jewish tradition, the roads to these cities were kept in excellent condition, with large, visible signs reading *"Refuge! Refuge!"* pointing the way. Obstacles were removed, and bridges were built to aid those running for their lives. The gates to these cities always remained unlocked. Each of the six cities (three on each side of the Jordan) was strategically placed so that no one was too far from safety.

Anyone, regardless of ethnicity, status, or background, could flee there. These cities were open to all.

Psalm 46:1 tells us, "God is our refuge and strength, an very present help in trouble." The cities of refuge point us to the heart of God, and they also challenge us:

- Are we making the way to the Gospel clear and accessible?
- Do we remove barriers for those seeking hope and healing?
- Do we build bridges to Christ or walls of judgment?
- Do our churches shout *"Refuge!"* or whisper exclusion?

The Gospel is for all people. As Ephesians 2 reminds us, God has broken down the dividing walls of hostility. We must follow His lead, ensuring that every ethnicity, every background, and every broken person hears the invitation to come and find mercy.

Justice with Mercy

Each city of refuge was home to the Levites trained in God's law. These leaders ensured that justice was done rightly. When someone arrived, he stood at the gate and explained his case. If the death was unintentional, the city would take him in. But if the person came with murder in his heart, he was turned away. These cities were not sanctuaries for the guilty but refuges for the innocent, for those who killed without intent.

Even then, life was still valued deeply. The person had to remain in the city until the death of the high priest. Though unintentional, a life had been lost, and there were consequences. God values **truth**, **accuracy**, and **due process**.

Deuteronomy 19:5 gives an example: A man is chopping wood, and the axe head flies off and kills his neighbor. That was an accident, not murder, but it was still serious. God's laws protected the manslayer while upholding the sanctity of life.

These cities also demonstrate equal treatment. Foreigners and sojourners were given the same rights as native Israelites. God provided justice and mercy for all because all are made in His image.

The Message for Us

The cities of refuge reflect the heart of God.

- He provides **safety.**
- He pursues **justice.**
- He offers **mercy.**
- He values **life**, every life.

Let us be people who reflect the same. May we build lives and churches that point clearly to our refuge in Christ. May we create spaces that welcome the broken and apply God's truth with wisdom, accuracy, and compassion.

Let's make the signs large, the paths clear, and the doors open. Because God values **justice and mercy**—so should we.

> **COURAGEOUS STEP:**
>
> Take an action today to reflect God's justice and mercy in your life. Forgive someone who doesn't deserve it. Extend kindness to a stranger. Advocate for the vulnerable. Speak up for those who can't speak for themselves. No ideas yet? Call your local pregnancy center or homeless shelter and ask to volunteer for a day.

Living Among the People

Joshua 21:3, 41–42: "So by command of the Lord the people of Israel gave to the Levites the following cities and pasturelands out of their inheritance ... The cities of the Levites in the midst of the possession of the people of Israel were in all forty-eight cities with their pasturelands. These cities each had its pasturelands around it. So it was with all these cities."

The **Levites lived among the people**.

What remarkable wisdom is displayed in God's design. The Levites, Israel's priestly tribe, did not receive a central region of their own like the other tribes. Instead, they were scattered throughout the land and placed in **48 cities** across Israel, including the **six cities of refuge**. This was not random. It was intentional.

In the cities of refuge, Levites served a crucial judicial function. They knew God's law and were equipped to determine whether a person had committed premeditated murder or accidental manslaughter. Their presence ensured that justice and mercy were upheld according to God's will.

In the other 48 cities, the Levites lived with pasturelands for livestock, animals that would be needed for sacrifices. And because these cities were dispersed throughout Israel, no standing army was needed to defend a separate Levite territory. Scholars estimate that **no Israelite lived more than ten miles** from one of the Levite towns. That meant wherever someone lived, **access to someone who knew and taught God's law was never far away.**

This strategic distribution reminds us of the importance of **local churches** and **faithful teachers** spread across every region and nation. People need regular access to the Word of God, clearly explained and faithfully lived out.

That's why we **plant churches.**
That's why we **send missionaries.**
That's why we support the **Great Commission.**

God's design hasn't changed. Just as the Levites were distributed among the people, we need **pastors, shepherds, teachers, and disciple-makers** distributed throughout the world. Every town, every culture, every language needs access to the Gospel.

Do you support **church planting**?
Do you pray for **missions**?
Do you give? Do you go? Do you encourage others?

Whether you travel overseas, serve locally, support financially, or pray faithfully, **we all have a role to play** in spreading the good news. As Paul said, *"How are they to hear without someone preaching?"* And how will someone preach unless they are sent?

There's another profound layer to this passage. In Genesis 49:7, Jacob rebukes Simeon and Levi for their violence at Shechem: *"I will divide them in Jacob and scatter them in Israel."* It seemed like a curse. But later, in Exodus 32:25–29, the tribe of Levi responded to Moses' call, standing with the Lord against idolatry. Because of their zeal, they were ordained for service.

Simeon was scattered and faded. The Levites were also scattered but elevated. God redeemed their past and transformed their scattering into a sacred calling.

That's grace.

And that grace didn't end with them. The Levites now lived among the people not only to administer sacrifices but to **share the message of grace**.

Finally, remember this: In Joshua 13:14, 33 and 18:7, we're told that the Lord Himself was the Levites' inheritance. They didn't receive land like the other tribes because they received something greater—a relationship with the living God.

That points us forward beyond this land in which we live.

We, too, are called to live among the people, not storing up earthly inheritance but holding fast to a better one. *"The city that has foundations, whose designer and builder is God"* (Hebrews 11:10).

Let's live grounded in grace, scattered with purpose, and focused on an eternal inheritance.

COURAGEOUS STEP:

Share your faith with someone. If that terrifies you, just tell someone your story. Tell them how you came to know the Lord. We are commanded to make disciples. If you can't do that verbally yet, then write a note to someone sharing your story or post your testimony on social media. Wherever you are, take a step toward becoming comfortable sharing your faith. Realize that you aren't responsible for the results. You are only responsible for being faithful to share. The rest is up to God.

God Keeps His Promises

Joshua 21:43–45: "Thus the Lord gave to Israel all the land that he swore to give to their fathers. And they took possession of it, and they settled there. And the Lord gave them rest on every side just as he had sworn to their fathers. Not one of all their enemies had withstood them, for the Lord had given all their enemies into their hands. Not one word of all the good promises that the Lord had made to the house of Israel had failed; all came to pass."

Not one word failed.

This theme echoes throughout these devotions because it echoes throughout Joshua and all of God's Word. Repetition matters. It exists for our benefit because we are prone to forget. We forget that **God is trustworthy**. We default to leaning on our own understanding or the fleeting answers this world offers. But scripture reminds us again and again: *God's Word never fails.*

As the conquest narrative pauses before Joshua's final speeches, the author intentionally reminds us of something vital:

- God gave the land, *just as He promised.*
- God gave victory over their enemies, *just as He promised.*
- God gave rest, *just as He promised.*
- And *not one word* of His good promises failed.

How many times must we hear this truth before we really believe it?

God is patient. He told Abraham that the land wouldn't be given in his lifetime. He waited centuries for the iniquity of the Amorites to reach full measure before bringing judgment. He allowed Joseph to die in Egypt with nothing but the hope that his bones would one day be carried into the Promised Land. Generations waited. But **God kept every promise.**

He still does.

He has promised to forgive our sins if we confess and repent. He has promised to never leave us nor forsake us. He has promised to make all things new, to wipe away every tear, and to give us life as it was meant to be.

Yet how often do we still doubt Him?

God has parted the waters—literally. He has stood up waters, stopped the sun, shattered city walls, silenced armies, and raised the dead. He has controlled the rise and fall of nations and kings. He has done everything He said He would do.

What more do we need?

Satan, the father of lies, has been deceiving people since Eden. He convinced Eve to doubt God's Word. That deception cost Adam and Eve their place in paradise and their direct communion with God. And he hasn't stopped. He still prowls like a roaring lion, seeking to devour. He still whispers lies into our hearts and minds.

Scripture is clear: We were dead in our sins, deceived by the Devil, drifting with the world, depraved in our conduct, and doomed in our destination. **But God,** rich in mercy, saved us. He raised us up and seated us in heavenly places with Christ.

God has kept every promise. The question is: **will you finally trust Him?**

Will you continue chasing the emptiness of this world, believing its hollow promises and finding only vanity and dissatisfaction? How many more times must your plans fall apart before you surrender and admit that your way doesn't work?

When will we finally learn that *God keeps His promises*?

The sooner we realize that God created us with purpose, that He loves us with a love beyond comprehension, and that His promises never fail, the sooner we will begin to flourish in the life He designed for us, both now and forever.

Scripture testifies.
History testifies.
I testify to you: **God keeps His promises.**

Will you trust Him today?

COURAGEOUS STEP:

Scripture has reminded us that God keeps His promises again for a reason. Choose to memorize another promise of God and pray through that promise this week, asking the Lord to help you believe it and trust in Him.

Turn and Go: Wisdom for Living

Joshua 22:5–6: "'Only be very careful to observe the commandment and the law that Moses the servant of the Lord commanded you, to love the Lord your God, and to walk in all his ways and to keep his commandments and to cling to him and to serve him with all your heart and with all your soul.' So Joshua blessed them and sent them away, and they went to their tents."

Most parents know the feeling of sending their children off—whether it's the first day of school, college move-in day, or walking them down the aisle at their wedding. These are significant, often emotional moments, and in them, we tend to give parting words of wisdom as life instructions that we hope will stick.

In Joshua 22, we see a similar scene. After seven long years of intense battle, Joshua is sending home the eastern tribes, faithful soldiers who fought alongside their fellow Israelites. Joshua knows he may never see them again. These are his final words to them, and they represent his most important instruction.

Joshua commends before he commands.

This principle is worth noting. Before giving instructions, Joshua expresses appreciation and honor. In leadership, and especially in relationships, people are more likely to listen when they know they are valued. Too often, we take appreciation for granted and emphasize correction. Joshua models a better way: commendation builds the bridge for instruction.

Then comes the heart of his message in verse 6: *"Be very careful to observe the commandment and the law."* But he doesn't stop there. He gives five specific actions that explain what careful obedience looks like:

1. Love the Lord your God.

Love is the starting point. Joshua doesn't aim for behavior modification; he calls for heart transformation. Everything begins with love for God.

2. Walk in all His ways.

This image is rich. Walking with God means steady, daily movement like a child walking through the woods with a parent, learning to notice beauty, avoid danger, and follow the right path. We discover that God's ways are best and that His commands lead to life.

3. Keep His commandments.

This assumes we know His Word. We can't keep what we haven't read. Joshua echoes his earlier instruction from chapter 1:8: *"Meditate on the law day and night."* A good rule to live by: **No Bible, no breakfast. No scripture, no sleep.** Let God's Word be your first and final thought each day.

4. Cling to Him.

Cling to God like misapplied superglue binds two fingers, inseparably. In hardship and joy, on mountaintops and in valleys, we cling to Him. He is our refuge, our strength, and our anchor.

5. Serve Him with all your heart and soul.

Joshua ends where he began with wholehearted love. Service flows from affection. God doesn't want half-hearted duty; He wants devotion with all your heart.

Joshua's wisdom rings true for us today. As we "turn and go" into the rhythms of everyday life, into work, family, ministry, decisions, and challenges, God's words remain relevant.

1. Love God.
2. Walk with Him.
3. Keep His Word.
4. Cling to Him.
5. Serve Him with all your heart and soul.

This is wisdom for living. It's how we flourish, how we stay faithful, and how we pass on the faith to those who follow us.

So as you step into whatever God has called you to today, take these five truths with you. Live them. Share them. And never forget—God walks with those who walk with Him.

> **COURAGEOUS STEP:**
>
> Evaluate your heart. Which one of these five commands do you need to focus on the most? Circle that one. Now focus on keeping it this week.

Misunderstandings

Joshua 22:22b, 24: "If it was in rebellion or in breach of faith against the Lord, do not spare us today . . . No, but we did it from fear that in time to come your children might say to our children, 'What have you to do with the Lord, the God of Israel?'"

The tribes west of the Jordan misunderstood the eastern tribes' intentions. They saw the large altar built near the Jordan and assumed it was a rebellious attempt to bypass the Lord's command. According to Deuteronomy 12:13–14, sacrifices were only to be offered at the place the Lord had chosen. This act, if it were indeed rebellion, would have been a serious breach of covenant faithfulness—one that, as they reminded each other, could bring judgment upon all of Israel.

The western tribes sent Phinehas, a priest known for his zeal for God's holiness, to confront what they believed was a serious offense. In his plea, Phinehas recalled the sin of Achan, which cost 36 lives, and the rebellion at Peor, where twenty-four thousand died in a plague. The situation was serious, and they were prepared for war.

But then came the explanation.

The eastern tribes never intended to rebel. Their altar wasn't for sacrifice at all. Instead, it was a memorial, a witness for future generations. They feared that one day, the descendants of the western tribes might say to their children, "You don't belong to the Lord." So, they built a symbol to preserve unity, a visible reminder that both sides served the same God.

This is where Proverbs 18:17 comes to life: "The one who states his case first seems right, until the other comes and examines him."

We can all relate. We hear one side of a story and are quick to form opinions. We often assume the worst about others' motives. And while we give ourselves the benefit of the doubt, we're slow to extend that same grace to others.

Look closely at how the eastern tribes responded to unjust accusations.

They could have reacted with resentment. They had just spent seven years fighting shoulder-to-shoulder with the western tribes to conquer a land they wouldn't even inhabit. And now they were being accused of betrayal?

But instead of anger, they answered with **gentleness** and **humility**. They reminded their brothers of their loyalty, clarified their intentions, and reaffirmed their shared commitment to the Lord.

Proverbs 15:1 reminds us, "A soft answer turns away wrath, but a harsh word stirs up anger."

Even more striking is where they built the altar: on the western side of the Jordan. If their goal had been convenience in worship, they would have placed it on their own side. Instead, they built it where it would be visible to both sides, a powerful sign of unity and shared faith.

Both sides in this story were zealous for God. Both wanted to preserve faithfulness and holiness. But a **misunderstanding nearly led to civil war.**

And if we're honest, we've been there, too.

We've misread someone's actions. We've assumed motives. We've held grudges or pulled away from people based on assumptions rather than conversations. We've avoided direct dialogue, allowing fear, suspicion, or offense to grow in our hearts.

This passage teaches us several important lessons:

- **One side of the story isn't the whole story.**
- **Face-to-face conversations can prevent relational disaster.**
- **Gentle words de-escalate tension.**
- **Reconciliation is worth the effort even when it costs us something.**

The western tribes even offered to give up land so their eastern brothers could live closer to the tabernacle. That's a costly step toward reconciliation.

Let's follow their example.

Let's seek peace with one another. Let's talk instead of assuming. Let's offer gentle answers instead of harsh reactions. And when misunderstandings arise, as they surely will, let's pursue unity in Christ and restore relationships for the sake of the Gospel.

> **COURAGEOUS STEP:**
>
> If there is a strained relationship in your life, choose to take the first step toward forgiveness and, if it doesn't put you in harm's way, reconciliation. Make a mental note that next time conflict arises, you will go directly to the source and not believe rumors.

What About Our Children?

Joshua 22:25: "For the Lord has made the Jordan a boundary between us and you, you people of Reuben and people of Gad. You have no portion in the Lord.' So your children might make our children cease to worship the Lord."

The eastern tribes built an altar of imposing size, not out of rebellion, but out of concern for their **children**. They built a **witness** for future generations, knowing a natural divide like the Jordan River could one day become a spiritual and relational divide.

And honestly, I admire their foresight.

These men had personally experienced the power and faithfulness of God. They had seen the Jordan's waters stand in a heap. They had marched around Jericho and watched its walls fall. They saw the sun stand still, hailstones fall from heaven, and hornets drive out enemy warriors. They had lived through seven years of miraculous victories and God's unshakable promises.

But their children wouldn't have those same firsthand memories. They express concern about future generations forgetting. They asked what if your children say to ours, *"You have no portion in the* Lord*"?* (Joshua 22:27). So they built an altar, not to offer sacrifices, but to say: **"We belong to Yahweh, too."**

Was it the best solution? Maybe not. But **at least they did something** to bridge the gap between generations. And their motivation is something we should take seriously.

Scripture gives us a clearer plan in Deuteronomy 6:6–7: "And these words that I command you today shall be on your heart. You shall teach them diligently to your children, and shall talk of them when you sit in your house, and when you walk by the way, and when you lie down, and when you rise."

The command is clear. We don't just pass along faith casually—we do it intentionally and consistently. Faith isn't taught only in sermons or Sunday School. It's passed along in conversations at the dinner table, in prayers before bed, in talks on the way to school, and in open Bibles shared together in the morning.

So, what are we doing to pass our faith to the next generation?

At **Cedarville University**, where I serve, this is why we exist.

College is a critical moment when students begin to own their faith, make independent decisions, and set the trajectory for their future. The world is eager to shape the next generation with a secular, humanistic, godless worldview.

But **we want them to know the truth:**

- That God created the world in six literal days.
- That He sent His Son to die for their sins.
- That Jesus rose again, conquering sin and death.
- That salvation is by grace alone, through faith alone, in Christ alone, for the glory of God alone.

We want them to know the miracles of God.

We want them to understand the truth and own their faith.

We want to prepare them to live lives of wisdom, planted like trees beside streams of living water, bearing fruit in due season (Psalm 1).

At Cedarville, **we stand for the Word of God and the Testimony of Jesus Christ.** We aim to transform lives through excellent education and intentional discipleship under biblical authority.

This is our calling.

This is our mission.

This is our answer to the question: **"what about our children?"**

I ask you: **Will you join us?** Because every generation has the responsibility to reach the next with clarity, compassion, and conviction.

That journey begins with a simple but powerful question: **what about our children?**

> **COURAGEOUS STEP:**
>
> Choose an appropriate action to pass along your faith to the next generation. If you are a parent, tell your children a story about God's faithfulness in your life. No children? Volunteer to mentor someone or serve in the youth or children's ministry at your local church.

A Legacy of Faithful Witness

Joshua 22:26–27a; 34: "Therefore we said, 'Let us now build an altar, not for burnt offering, nor for sacrifice, but to be a witness between us and you, and between our generations after us'... The people of Reuben and the people of Gad called the altar Witness, 'For,' they said, 'it is a witness between us that the Lord is God.'"

In a courtroom, **a witness testifies to what they have seen or heard.** In the context of faith, a witness testifies to **what they know to be true about God**—His character, His work, and His Word.

In Joshua 22, the tribes of Reuben, Gad, and the half-tribe of Manasseh build a massive altar, not for sacrifices, but as a memorial. It was intended to be a witness across generations. A reminder:

- To the eastern tribes that worship was to occur at the one true altar God had established.
- To the western tribes that their eastern brothers worshipped the same God and belonged fully to the covenant community.

The Jordan River formed a natural boundary. The altar, described as "of imposing size," served as a bridge across that divide, a visible call to unity in worship of the one true God (Joshua 22:10).

This was a beautiful intention. A generation that had experienced God's power firsthand—the parting of the Jordan, the fall of Jericho, hailstorms from heaven, the sun standing still—wanted to ensure that future generations would remain faithful.

But something went wrong.

We only have to turn the page to the book of Judges to see that Israel failed. The generations that followed *"did not know the Lord or the works He had done for Israel"* (Judges 2:10). The monument remained, but the message faded.

What do we learn?

A legacy of faithful witness doesn't come from silent monuments, no matter how grand. **A faithful witness comes from intentional discipleship, faithful teaching, and relational investment in the next generation.**

We must tell the next generation what God has done.
We must teach them who God is.
We must model for them what it means to walk with Him daily.

At Cedarville, we call this season of life the greenhouse, a temporary, protected space where students grow deep roots of faith before being planted in the world. We desire to see them graduate as Psalm 1 Christians, rooted by streams of living water, bearing fruit in due season.

But growth like that doesn't happen automatically.

It requires:

- Owning one's faith
- Walking with God daily
- Living in authentic Christian community
- Pursuing spiritual disciplines
- Serving faithfully in strong local churches

A legacy of faithful witness isn't left through a tattoo, a necklace, a painting, or even a monument. It's left through the **lives of people** who have been **transformed by the Gospel** and who are now **investing in others.**

2 Timothy 2:2 says, "What you have heard from me in the presence of many witnesses entrust to faithful men, who will be able to teach others also."

That's the legacy that lasts.

So, let me ask you:

- Are you investing in the next generation?
- Are you passing on the truth of God's Word to someone younger than you?
- Are you building your legacy in monuments or in **witnesses**?

Let's not spend our lives constructing things that can't speak. **Let's invest in people who will testify to the faithfulness of God long after we're gone.**

When we do that, we don't just build a monument; we build a **legacy of faithful witness.**

COURAGEOUS STEP:

Choose the appropriate next step(s) for you:

1. Own your faith and understand what you believe.
2. Walk with God daily through reading and meditating on scripture.
3. Pray (talk to God) regularly.
4. Serve in your local church.

Be Strong and Careful

Joshua 23:6: "Therefore, be very strong to keep and to do all that is written in the Book of the Law of Moses, turning aside from it neither to the right hand nor to the left."

At the end of his life, Joshua repeats the words the Lord gave him at the beginning of his leadership journey. Do you hear the echo?

"Be very strong."

"Do all that is written."

"Do not turn from it to the right or to the left."

These are not new words. They're the same instructions God gave Joshua in Joshua 1:7, "Only be strong and very courageous, being careful to do according to all the law ... Do not turn from it to the right hand or to the left."

Joshua had learned through decades of leading Israel that **God keeps His promises** and that God's way is always best. Now, as he prepares to pass the baton, he urges the next generation of leaders to cling to the same truth that carried him: God's Word is trustworthy. Stay faithful to it.

We live in a world obsessed with novelty. Creativity is often praised more than faithfulness. In ministry, in theology, and even in personal discipleship, we can feel pressure to be clever, original, or innovative. But God has not called us to be inventors. He has called us to be faithful stewards of His truth.

The Gospel is not new. The call to obedience is not new. We are not to chase after trendy ideas or the "next big thing." As Solomon reminds us in Ecclesiastes 1:9: "There is nothing new under the sun." We are called to proclaim the old, old story of Jesus and His love, faithfully, boldly, and without compromise.

Cling to the Lord

In this same passage, Joshua urges Israel's leaders to cling to the Lord. Why? Because humans are worshippers by design. The question is never *if* we'll worship, but *what* or *whom* we will worship.

In Joshua 23:12, Joshua warns that if they turn back and cling to the remnants of the nations around them, judgment will follow. But if they cling to the Lord, they will walk in blessing.

We face the same choice. To cling to the Lord means finding our identity in Christ, not in the world. As Paul teaches in Ephesians, we are no longer in Adam but in Christ. We have put off the old self and put on the new. We are no longer darkness but light. That changes everything.

We don't cling to false gods anymore, not material possessions, not addictions, not success, not comfort or pleasure or performance. We cling to the One who conquered all those things.

Jesus broke our chains. He forgave us. He redeemed us. He justified us. He will glorify us and raise us. Why would we ever return to the very things He came to rescue us from?

And yet, we often do.

We seek comfort in bottles, pills, screens, relationships, or food. But those are just modern-day idols, cheap substitutes for the true refuge of our souls.

The answer? **Renew your mind daily**. Walk with the Lord. Cling to Him in joy and sorrow, in victory and defeat.

Maturity means clinging to Christ.

Maybe as a child, you had a blanket or stuffed animal that brought comfort. You clung to it. Over time, you outgrew it. You matured.

In the same way, spiritual maturity means letting go of the things we once clung to and learning to cling only to the Lord. To walk in His ways. To not veer off to the right or the left.

But that doesn't happen passively. As Joshua says, we must be very strong to keep God's commands.

So, cling to the Lord. Cling to His Word. Cling to the unchanging truth in an ever-changing world.

You will never regret it.

> **COURAGEOUS STEP:**
> Choose today to cling to Christ. Write down the situation in your life that causes you the most fear, anxiety, and despair. Choose to cling to Christ during those moments. Ask Him for help. If needed, keep a reminder nearby, like a coin in your pocket, a bracelet, a necklace, or something similar.

The Way of All the Earth

Joshua 23:14: "And now I am about to go the way of all the earth, and you know in your hearts and souls, all of you, that not one word has failed of all the good things that the Lord your God promised concerning you. All have come to pass for you; not one of them has failed."

In his second farewell address, Joshua speaks plainly to the leaders of Israel, *"I am about to go the way of all the earth."*

He is nearing death, and he knows it. But before he departs, he offers something better than a final wish; he gives his **life testimony**.

"You know in your hearts and souls . . . that not one word has failed of all the good things that the Lord your God promised concerning you. All have come to pass."

What a powerful statement. At the end of a long and faithful life, Joshua doesn't offer regrets or apologies. He doesn't lament missed opportunities. Instead, he offers a bold declaration: **God has kept every single promise.**

> **God has kept every single promise.**

Joshua could say this with authority. He had lived it:

- He had served Moses with humility.
- He had crossed the Jordan on dry ground.
- He had seen the walls of Jericho fall and watched God conquer armies with hailstones.
- He had witnessed the sun stand still in the sky.
- He had seen victory through obedience and failure through sin.
- He had experienced deception but also God's redemption of mistakes.
- He had stood by Caleb as the giants fell and the land was claimed.

And at the end of it all, he testified: **God is faithful. You can trust Him.**

We will all go the way of the earth.

Joshua's words are not just poetic; they are profoundly universal. "The way of all the earth" is the path we will all walk. Death is the great equalizer. No matter your strength, wealth, intellect, or success, **you will die.** So will I.

The book of Joshua begins with the death of Moses and ends with the deaths of Joshua, Eleazar, and a reminder of Joseph's death. Their legacies were different, but the end was the same.

When you're young, you don't think about death. You shake off injuries. You assume time is on your side. But as the years pass, your body reminds you that you're not invincible.

I've seen it on our college campus—young lives taken too soon. I once led a memorial service for a student, and one young man cried loudly and uncontrollably throughout the entire service. It was a visceral reminder: **Death does not seem right**. It's not how things were meant to be.

We were made to live. But **sin entered the world**, and through sin came death. We are not just victims of Adam's rebellion. We are participants. Every one of us has affirmed Adam's sin with our own.

And so, *we too will go the way of all the earth.*

Are you ready?

That's the real question. Not if, but when, and *are you ready?*

If you've never repented of your sin and placed your faith in Jesus Christ, then scripture says judgment awaits. You will be found guilty and separated from God for eternity. But there is good news.

Jesus Christ took your place. He bore your sin. He died your death. He satisfied the justice of God and rose from the grave.

If you repent by turning from your sin and trusting in Christ, you will be saved by God's grace. God will no longer see your guilt. He will see the righteousness of Christ credited to your account.

You will be justified, forgiven, adopted, and made new. You will not fear death because Christ has conquered it.

I'm ready. Are you?

I don't fear going the way of all the earth. Because I know what waits on the other side: resurrection. There is nothing this world can do to me that resurrection glory won't fix.

I ask you today: **Are you ready to go the way of all the earth?** Have you trusted in Jesus Christ? Can you say with confidence what Joshua said: *"Not one word of the Lord has failed"*?

If not, I pray that **today is the day of salvation.**

Repent. Believe. Follow Christ. And live with confidence until the day you, too, go the way of all the earth and rise again to eternal life.

> **COURAGEOUS STEP:**
>
> Live with eternity in view. Are you ready? You will die one day. First, make sure you know Jesus. Then ask, what is my life testifying to others about what I believe? Identify and act upon one way you can invest in something of eternal value this week.

Shechem—A Memorable Place

Joshua 24:1a: "Joshua gathered all the tribes of Israel to Shechem."

Why Shechem?

Of all the places Joshua could have chosen for his final covenant renewal with Israel, he chose Shechem. Why? Because **Shechem was not just a location; it was a place rich with spiritual history and deep covenantal significance.**

Approximately **six hundred years earlier,** God made a promise to Abraham that He would give his descendants the land of Canaan. That promise? It was made in Shechem (Genesis 12:6). The land they now stood on was the land God had first pledged so many generations ago.

Later, Jacob, after fleeing from Esau, returned safely to the land of Canaan. When he arrived, he came to the city of Shechem, and there he built an altar and called it *"El-Elohe-Israel"* or "God, the God of Israel" (Genesis 33:20). God had preserved him, and Jacob acknowledged it in worship. But there's more.

In preparation for that moment of worship, Jacob told his family, "Put away the foreign gods that are among you, purify yourselves, and change your garments." They did. They handed over their idols and earrings, and Jacob **buried them under a tree near Shechem** (Genesis 35). Shechem became **a place of cleansing,** a place of commitment, and a place of obedience.

It was also **a place of hope fulfilled.** Joseph's bones, carried out of Egypt, were buried at Shechem on the land Jacob had bought. It became an inheritance for Joseph's descendants. Joseph had trusted that God would keep His promise, even though he never saw it with his own eyes. His hope was not in vain.

Joshua chose Shechem for this final gathering of the tribes strategically. He wanted Israel to remember. God made a promise at Shechem. God kept that promise. And now, standing in the very place where that covenant began, Joshua called Israel to respond with obedience, faithfulness, and renewed worship.

What can we learn?

First, **God is not in a hurry**.

It took **six hundred years** for the promise to Abraham to be fulfilled. God allowed centuries for the iniquity of the Amorites to reach full measure. Abraham, Isaac, Jacob, and Joseph never saw the fulfillment in their lifetime. But they believed, and their faith was not misplaced.

Second, **God keeps His Word.**

Not one promise failed. Not one word was forgotten. Every part came to pass exactly as God said it would.

Third, **we can trust God with our future**, even if we don't see everything now.

I will likely go to the grave without seeing the return of Jesus. But I still believe. I still hope. Why? Because God kept His promise to Abraham, and He will keep His promises to me. He will return. He will resurrect the dead. He will make all things new. He will conquer evil forever.

Revisit your Shechems.

Every now and then, I visit my own "Shechems"—places where God has answered prayer, brought clarity, opened doors, or reminded me of His presence. These places matter. They aren't sacred because of geography but because of how they remind us about God.

You probably have Shechems, too.

- A quiet corner where you surrendered your life to Christ.
- A camp, a chapel, a hospital room, or a kitchen table where God met you.
- A place where tears fell, prayers were answered, or healing began.

These are not just memories. **These places testify to the fact that God is faithful. You can trust Him.**

COURAGEOUS STEP:

Revisit your Shechem. If you can't physically go there, then go there in your mind. Remember a place where God made Himself known to you or answered a prayer or supplied for a need. Journal or tell someone else about it to encourage your faith and theirs.

Put Away Other Gods

Joshua 24:14b: "Put away the gods that your fathers served beyond the River and in Egypt, and serve the Lord."

The word **exclusive** means limiting or limited to possession, control, or use by a single individual or group. And **Christianity's most controversial claim,** both in Joshua's day and in ours, is the **exclusivity of Jesus Christ.**

Many people around the world are happy to include Jesus in their spiritual framework if they don't have to **exclude** their other beliefs. But the message of scripture is not *"add Jesus to your life"*—it's *"repent and believe."* The call to faith is a call to **abandon all other gods.**

That's exactly what Joshua challenged Israel to do. In his final speech, he didn't just ask the people to believe in God. He called them to **put away the gods of their ancestors, of Egypt, and of the Amorites** and to serve the Lord alone.

Let that sink in! Even after the Jordan River stopped flowing, the walls of Jericho fell down, the sun stood still, and hailstones crushed their enemies, some Israelites still held onto foreign gods.

Seriously? After all they had seen, they still clung to idols?

Yes. And so do we.

We may not worship statues or golden calves, but we still serve **false gods,** just with different names: **money, comfort, sexual gratification, reputation, power, pleasure, approval,** or **control.**

The idols are more subtle but just as enslaving. What we love most—what we think about, what we spend our time and resources on, what shapes our decisions—reveals our true object of worship.

Who sits on the throne of your heart?

Whatever occupies the throne of your affections is your god. So we must ask hard questions:

- Where do I spend the bulk of my time, treasure, and talents?
- Do I idolize sports, social media, comfort, or achievement?
- Do I derive my identity, meaning, or security from something other than God?

Joshua's call is clear: **Put away your other gods. Serve the Lord only.**

This is the same decision Rahab made. When she hid the spies, she aligned herself with the God of Israel and turned away from the gods, culture, and security of her past. That's real repentance. That's the exclusive call of biblical faith.

The Commands Are Clear

In Joshua 24:14–15, the people are confronted with five commands:

- Fear the Lord.
- Serve Him in sincerity and faithfulness.
- Put away the foreign gods.
- Serve the Lord.
- Choose this day whom you will serve.

This is not passive faith. This is active, intentional surrender.

It reminds me of the old saying by Hudson Taylor, *"Christ is either Lord of all, or is not Lord at all."*

So today, ask yourself:

- Am I merely adding Jesus to my life, or have I surrendered all?
- What gods do I need to put away?
- Will I follow Christ exclusively, no matter the cost?

The Gospel isn't just an invitation; it's a decision. It's not a spiritual supplement. It's a total allegiance to the only God who saves.

So **put away other gods.**

COURAGEOUS STEP:

Stop! Put everything else down. Ask the Holy Spirit to reveal any "other gods" in your life. Seriously! You know you have them. Something you spend time, resources, and thoughts on more than God. Now, repent. Surrender that idol to the Lord today. Ask the Lord to help you love Him more than you love anything else this world has to offer.

You Are Not Able!

Joshua 24:19: "But Joshua said to the people, 'You are not able to serve the Lord, for he is a holy God. He is a jealous God; he will not forgive your transgressions or your sins.'"

Wait . . . what?

After calling the people to choose whom they would serve, and after they confidently declared, "We will serve the Lord," Joshua hits them with a sharp and sobering truth: **"You are not able."**

It's not the kind of motivational speech we expect. It's not how to win friends and influence people. But it's true, and it's exactly what they needed to hear. And so do we.

We are not able.

Have you ever resolved to change, only to fall flat?

- You promised to eat better . . . but gave in to the dessert.
- You swore you'd break a habit . . . but relapsed under pressure.

- You said you'd stop sinning in a particular area . . . and yet it surfaced again.

Willpower is not enough.

Especially in a culture like ours, rooted in self-reliance, achievement, and personal effort, we are taught to believe, *"I've got this. I can do this on my own."* But that mindset leads only to frustration and failure.

That was Israel's story too.

Though they chose rightly in saying, *"We will serve the Lord,"* their history would soon tell a different tale. The very next book, Judges, describes their descent into a repeated cycle:

- Sin
- Judgment
- Desperation
- Deliverance
- Repeat

Eventually, their repeated rebellion led to exile from the land God had graciously given them.

This is our story too.

Like Israel, **we are not able** to live faithfully on our own. We fall. We fail. We sin. The Christian life is not about trying harder or checking more religious boxes. It's about recognizing our inability and **depending completely on God's grace and power.**

We are saved by grace through faith, not by works. And we are sanctified (the ongoing process of becoming like Christ) the same way: by grace through faith, not through legalistic effort.

This was Paul's struggle in Romans 7:19: "I do not do the good I want, but the evil I do not want is what I keep on doing."

Can you relate? The heart wants to obey, but the flesh is weak. So what's the answer?

The good news: You're not able, but God is.

The difference between us and ancient Israel is this: If you've trusted in Jesus Christ, the Holy Spirit now lives in you. We move from Romans 7 to Romans 8:1, "There is therefore now no condemnation for those who are in Christ Jesus."

> You're not able, but God is.

All of your sins—past, present, and future—are covered by the blood of Jesus. You have been justified, made right with God, and nothing can separate you from His love. So do we keep on sinning because grace covers it? Absolutely not.

We learn to **walk with God**. We speak to Him in **prayer**. We renew our minds by meditating on His **Word**. We wage war against sin, not in our strength, but in **His strength**.

We will stumble. We will fall. But we don't stay down. We get up, not because *we are able*, but because **He is able**.

Don't focus on your inability—focus on His sufficiency

Yes, Joshua was right. **You are not able.** But the Gospel message is this: **Jesus is.**

- He lived the life we could not live.
- He died the death we deserved.
- He conquered sin, death, and the grave.

And now, through His Spirit, we are made able to follow Him, not perfectly, but persistently.

So don't fix your eyes on your failures. Fix them on your faithful Savior. Don't dwell on your sin. Dwell on His grace. Don't live in defeat. Live in the power of His resurrection.

Because in Christ, what once was impossible is now reality.

We are able because He is.

> **COURAGEOUS STEP:**
>
> Humility. It matters. Pray, "Lord, I can't, but you can." Choose to depend on the Spirit today. When you sense pride rising up within you, or when you are tempted to defend how good you are at something . . . stop. And remember that pride comes before the fall, but God exalts the humble. Here is my frequent prayer, "God, be merciful to me, a sinner." Feel free to make it yours too.

Choose Whom You Will Serve

Joshua 24:14–15: "Now therefore fear the Lord and serve him in sincerity and in faithfulness. Put away the gods that your fathers served beyond the River and in Egypt, and serve the Lord. And if it is evil in your eyes to serve the Lord, choose this day whom you will serve ... But as for me and my house, we will serve the Lord."

The word **"serve"** appears at least **sixteen times** in this chapter. The driving question comes in verse 15 and demands a personal response:

"Whom will you serve?"

Notice what's not in question: *whether* we will serve or worship. God created mankind to worship, and **we will worship something.** The only question is, *what or whom will we serve?*

Remember God's grace in the past.

Before issuing this challenge, Joshua recounts God's incredible grace toward Israel. He reminds them of the covenant at Shechem. He recalls how even Abraham once served other gods, yet God graciously called him out and made a promise to him. Joshua also references Jacob, Moses, the plagues in Egypt, the Red Sea, Balaam, the Jordan River, Jericho, and the many victories in the Promised Land.

In every case, God was the one who acted. God did the work, not Israel. The question, then, is clear. Remembering all God has done, **whom will you serve?**

God has been gracious to us, too. This question isn't just for ancient Israel. It's for us as well. Ephesians 2 reminds us that we were dead in our trespasses and sins. But God, rich in mercy, made us alive in Christ. He raised us up and gave us a seat in the heavenly places. He saved us by grace through faith, not by our own efforts. Just as with Israel, God has done the work of salvation.

So again, the question comes:

"Whom will you serve?"

The necessity of God's grace in the future.

Israel responded to Joshua's challenge by declaring, *"We will serve the Lord."* But instead of celebrating, Joshua replies with startling honesty: *"You are not able to serve the Lord, for He is a holy God"* (Joshua 24:18-19). No applause. No congratulations. Instead, a sober warning that foreshadows the struggles ahead.

Joshua doesn't let them off the hook. He presses further: *"You are witnesses against yourselves"* (Joshua 24:22). The people made a covenant, and for a time, those who knew the Lord's work remained faithful (Joshua 24:31). But the generations that followed would not continue in that pattern.

We need God's grace too. If you've ever struggled with sin and failed, you're not alone. The Christian life is about progress, not perfection. **We need forgiveness and strength daily.**

But we have something Israel didn't: **the indwelling Holy Spirit**.

- The Spirit empowers us to overcome sin.
- He frees us from bondage.
- He enables us to live new lives in Christ.

The struggle is real, but so is the victory. Read and meditate on scripture. Pray daily for the Spirit's help. Join a local church and commit to authentic Christian community. Begin a long walk in the same direction, faithfully getting back up when you fall.

"Choose this day whom you will serve."

Not someday. **Today.**

It's the most important decision you'll ever make. And it's one you'll need to keep making every single day.

May we, like Joshua, boldly declare, *"As for me and my house, we will serve the Lord."*

COURAGEOUS STEP:

In this book, on a sticky note, or on the mirror where you get ready every morning, write down who you will serve. Do you choose God or something else? Now, in your thoughts, words, and deeds, seek to live like it by the power of the Spirit. Keep looking to Christ until you look like Christ.

The Bones of Joseph

Joshua 24:32: "As for the bones of Joseph, which the people of Israel brought up from Egypt, they buried them at Shechem, in the piece of land that Jacob bought from the sons of Hamor the father of Shechem for a hundred pieces of money. It became an inheritance of the descendants of Joseph."

Genesis tells us that **Joseph lived 110 years**. He saw his family grow and flourish through three generations. As he neared death, Joseph gathered his family and spoke with certainty, "God will visit you and bring you up out of this land to the land that he swore to Abraham, to Isaac, and to Jacob" (Genesis 50:24).

Then he made them swear an oath: *"Carry my bones up from here"* (Genesis 50:25).

A Dreamer, But More Than a Dreamer

Joseph was a dreamer. Remember the sheaves all bowing down to his sheaf? Remember the stars and sun and moon bowing down to him? But Joseph was more than a dreamer; **he was a believer**.

Joseph likely had the opportunity to be buried in a prestigious tomb in Egypt. He had saved the nation from seven years of famine. His wisdom had made Egypt rich. He was admired, respected, and perhaps revered. **But Joseph had other dreams.**

He did not desire a grand Egyptian tomb. He longed for home, not the land of Pharaoh, but the land God had promised. He wanted his bones buried in the soil of covenant promise, in the place where God had spoken to Abraham.

A Long Journey of Faith

Exodus 13 tells us that Moses took the bones of Joseph with him when Israel fled Egypt. For **40 years**, someone carried that box of bones through the wilderness. Through hunger, thirst, rebellion, and miracles . . . the coffin remained with them.

Can you picture the children asking, *"Daddy, why are we carrying that box?"*

And the answer: *"Because these bones believe in something."*

The bones of Joseph **testified to faith in the unseen**. Joseph never saw the Promised Land, but he was so confident in God's Word that he gave instructions for his burial as if they were already there. His bones preached a message: **God keeps His promises.**

The Bones Still Speak

Then came the day, after centuries of waiting, when Joseph's bones were finally laid to rest at Shechem, the very land Jacob had purchased, the very place God had made His promise to Abraham.

And I can imagine someone whispering over the grave, *"Joseph, you were right. God did it. He kept His Word."*

Hebrews 11:22 says, "By faith Joseph, at the end of his life, made mention of the exodus of the Israelites and gave directions concerning his bones."

His final act was not about burial; it was about belief. Not about a grave, but about God's glory.

But those bones will speak once more.

Because one day, **God will again keep His promises**. The baby born in a manger, Jesus, the Savior who conquered the grave, will return. And when He does, the bones of Joseph and the bones of all who trusted in the Lord **will rise**.

Our bones will proclaim together, *"Jesus is Lord, to the glory of God the Father."*

COURAGEOUS STEP:

You're ready. With the help of the Spirit living within you, you can live with strong and courageous faith. Think back to day one. You've made progress. Now, keep walking in this same direction. Keep meditating on scripture, keep serving God, keep speaking truth to yourself, know that God will keep His promises, and that God will be with you. Exercise your faith and continue to build your spiritual muscle. God is faithful. We can trust Him.

Three Funerals and One Great Hope

Joshua 24:29-30: "After these things Joshua the son of Nun, the servant of the Lord, died, being 110 years old. And they buried him in his own inheritance at Timnath-serah, which is in the hill country of Ephraim, north of the mountain of Gaash."

The book of Joshua begins with the death of Moses. It ends with the burial of Joseph's bones and Joshua's funeral. Can you imagine that funeral?

Stories Worth Telling

A nation mourns the loss of a legendary leader. One of his fellow warriors stands and speaks:

"I remember fighting beside Joshua against the Amalekites. When Moses' hands were lifted, we prevailed. Joshua was tireless. Loyal. Brave."

Another adds, "He was Moses' assistant. Faithful in little and faithful in much."

Maybe Caleb was there, too, Joshua's lifelong friend and fellow spy. The two stood together against the majority. They believed when others doubted. They had the courage to declare, *"God can give us this land."* Two old warriors, still standing, who lived to see the dream come true.

A father might have spoken next: "I'll never forget camping near the Jordan. The river was overflowing. I feared for my family. My kids were small. I was worried. But Joshua took my hand, looked me in the eye, and said, 'It's going to be okay. Consecrate yourselves, for tomorrow the Lord will do wonders among you.'

"And He did. The priests stepped into the muddy river, and the water stopped. The riverbed turned to dry ground. I crossed with my children, tears in my eyes, and I remembered Joshua's words: *'God is faithful. We can trust Him.'*"

Perhaps a priest spoke next: "When Joshua told us to march around Jericho and blow trumpets, I thought he had lost his mind. I even told him so. But he just looked at me and said, *'God is faithful. We can trust Him.'*

"We marched. They mocked. We kept going. Then came the seventh day. The seventh lap. We blew the trumpets, and the walls fell. I stood stunned, covered in dust and in disbelief. *God was faithful.*"

Then, someone surely said, "Do you remember that really long day?

"We marched all night to save the Gibeonites even though they had deceived us. Five armies waited. It made no sense. But Joshua was a man of his word. When we asked him why, he simply said, *'God is faithful. We can trust Him.'*

"And God was. Hailstones fell from heaven. The enemy fled. Then Joshua prayed: *'Sun, stand still!'* And it did. The day stretched out, and God gave us victory. That night, I couldn't sleep. I kept replaying the battle, the prayer, the miracle. *God was faithful.*"

No doubt, others recalled his final speeches urging them to pursue God with passion, cling to the Lord instead of idols, and choose this day whom they will serve. Of course, you can't forget Joshua's conclusion, *"As for me and my house, we will serve the Lord."* Someone surely reminded the crowd that Joshua declared, "*Not one word of all the good promises of the Lord had failed. All came to pass.*"

Perhaps someone asked, "What do we put on his tombstone?" The General, The Leader, The Conqueror, Moses' Successor?

No. One voice said softly, *"The Servant of the Lord."*

Yes. That's it. That's who Joshua was when he was Moses' assistant, when he was a warrior, when he was a spy, when he was a leader, when he was young, and when he was old. He was **"a servant of the Lord."** There is no higher title. No greater legacy. No more worthy aim—for Joshua or for us.

One Great Hope

So the book of Joshua closes with three funerals. Moses, Joshua, and Eleazar. But it does not close without hope.

Because those bones (those of Moses, Joshua, Eleazar, and Joseph) will rise again on resurrection day.

So until that day, let us live with one goal: to be nothing more, and nothing less, than a **servant of the Lord**.

> **COURAGEOUS STEP:**
>
> One last time. Have you repented of your sins, and do you believe that Jesus rose from the dead? If not, now is the time. If so, go tell someone your story. It's worth telling. Tell them about the great hope you have found in Jesus Christ.

Endnotes

1. "New Data on Gen Z-Perceptions of Pressure, Anxiety and Empowerment," Barna Group, January 28, 2021, https://www.barna.com/research/gen-z-success/.
2. "Lumina-Gallup State of Higher Education Research Hub," Gallup.com, February 9, 2023, https://www.gallup.com/analytics/644939/state-of-higher-education.aspx.

About the Author

Since 2013, Dr. Thomas White has served as President of Cedarville University, where he leads with a passion for biblical truth, academic excellence, and intentional discipleship. The son and grandson of faithful Baptist pastors, Dr. White grew up in the local church and felt called from a young age to continue his family's legacy of gospel ministry.

After earning his MDiv and PhD in systematic theology from Southeastern Baptist Theological Seminary, he served in leadership and teaching roles at Southwestern Seminary before God called him to Cedarville. At the heart of Dr. White's leadership is a desire to raise up a generation of bold, compassionate, biblically faithful men and women who will make a difference for Christ—wherever He calls them.

During his presidency, Cedarville has experienced remarkable growth, from launching the largest fundraising campaign in its history and growing in enrollment and new programs to building new spaces that serve students well. But his favorite moments involve mentoring students, opening God's Word in chapel, and encouraging young leaders to pursue Jesus wholeheartedly.

Dr. White is the author of a three-volume series on James Madison Pendleton and editor of *First Freedom: The Baptist Perspective on Religious Liberty* and *Upon This Rock*. He lives in Cedarville, Ohio, with his wife, Joy, their two children, and their dogs—where they love cheering for the Cedarville University Yellow Jackets and welcoming students into their home.

EVERY DAY MATTERS
PSALM 90:12

Choose today to deepen your walk with Christ and develop your professional skills when you join Cedarville's vibrant Christian learning community in person or online!

EXPLORE YOUR FUTURE:
CEDARVILLE.EDU

175+ programs to choose from ... all taught with academic excellence and a biblical worldview!

CEDARVILLE
UNIVERSITY.

for the **WORD OF GOD** and the **TESTIMONY** of **JESUS CHRIST**

Undergraduate | Graduate | Dual Enrollment

A student's **1000 DAYS** at Cedarville Begin With a

CAMPUS VISIT

Choose a CU Friday, an Academic Preview Day, or a personalized visit planned just for you:

cedarville.edu/visit

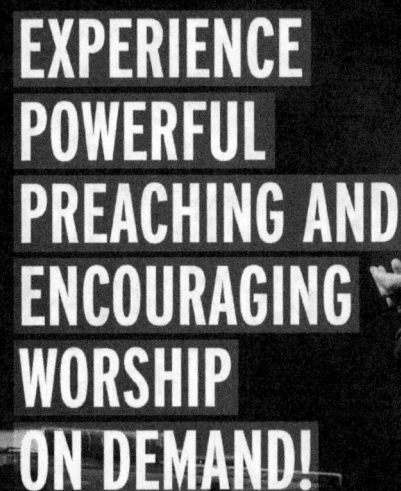

MAKE TIME FOR WHAT MATTERS MOST

Study the Bible with free online courses from trusted Cedarville faculty.

☑ BIBLE AND THE GOSPEL
The Bible and the Gospel is an introductory course on the nature of the Bible and how to study it inductively, along with biblical practices for growing in Christian maturity and embracing the Gospel-sharing mission.

☑ OLD TESTAMENT LITERATURE
Explore the history of the Hebrew nation from its origin to the time of Jesus Christ and see how the stories fit together in God's redemptive plan.

☑ NEW TESTAMENT LITERATURE
Survey the entire New Testament, including the historical background of the inter-testamental period, with special attention to key events, the authorship and literary genre of each book, and the unfolding of God's redemptive purpose through Jesus Christ.

☑ THEOLOGY I
Learn about the doctrines of the triune God, creation and humanity, revelation, and sin and discover how they relate to our lives today.

☑ THEOLOGY II
Learn about the doctrines of Christ, salvation, the Holy Spirit, and the last things and discover how they relate to our lives today.

cedarville.edu/StudytheBible

THIS BOOK IS PROTECTED INTELLECTUAL PROPERTY

The author of this book values Intellectual Property. The book you just read is protected by Instant IP^{IP}, a proprietary process, which integrates blockchain technology giving Intellectual Property "Global Protection." By creating a "Time-Stamped" smart contract that can never be tampered with or changed, we establish "First Use" that tracks back to the author.

Instant IP ^{IP} functions much like a Pre-Patent since it provides an immutable "First Use" of the Intellectual Property. This is achieved through our proprietary process of leveraging blockchain technology and smart contracts. As a result, proving "First Use" is simple through a global and verifiable smart contract. By protecting intellectual property with blockchain technology and smart contracts, we establish a "First to File" event.

Protected by Instant IP ^{IP}

LEARN MORE AT INSTANTIP.TODAY

www.ingramcontent.com/pod-product-compliance
Lightning Source LLC
Chambersburg PA
CBHW052137070526
44585CB00017B/1859